RANDOM HOUSE

Vacation

CROSSWORDS

Volume 1

Edited by Stanley Newman

**Random House
Puzzles & Games**

ISBN 0-8129-3289-7

Random House Puzzles & Games Web site address:
www.puzzlesatrandom.com

Page design and typography by Mark Frnka
Manufactured in the United States of America
8   9   7

SPECIAL SALES

Random House Puzzles & Games books are available at special discounts for
bulk purchases for sales promotions or premiums. Special editions, including
personalized covers, excerpts of existing books, and corporate imprints, can
be created in large quantities for special needs.
For more information, write to Random House, Inc., Special Markets/Premium
Sales, 1745 Broadway, MD 6-2, New York, NY, 16017 or
email: specialmarkets@randomhouse.com.

1 FRUITFUL

by Shirley Soloway

ACROSS
1 Alaskan island
5 Leading player
9 Set in
14 Bridle control
15 Have a drink
16 __ Loa
17 Strong brews
18 Felt sorry about
19 Stacked (up)
20 Fats Domino tune
23 Separated
24 Fortuneteller
25 Part of TGIF
28 Tie __ (cravat pins)
30 More costly
32 Traffic snarl
35 Kind of clam
38 "Put __ on it!"
40 Marsupial, for short
41 Matures
42 Application item
47 Matched pieces
48 Actor Estevez
49 1995, e.g.
51 Family pet
52 Cup edges
55 Notched, as a leaf
58 IBM competitor
62 __ Pass (Uris novel)
64 Spanish surrealist
65 Plantation of fiction
66 Fisherman's milieu
67 King or Young
68 Sponsorship
69 Pains in the neck
70 Singer k.d.
71 Like the Mariana Trench

DOWN
1 Jordanian, e.g.
2 "I cannot __ lie"
3 See 32 Across
4 Put out of office
5 Elongate
6 Guided trip
7 Imitators
8 Change color again
9 Realms
10 Post
11 Pond inhabitants
12 Chemical suffix
13 June celebrant
21 Bric-a-__
22 Actress Lamarr
26 Taylor of *The Nanny*
27 "__ my case"
29 Resident of Belgrade
31 __ glance
32 World-weary
33 Budget rival
34 Makes less severe
36 Louis XVI, e.g.
37 Actor Calhoun
39 Neighbor of Penna.
43 Crankcase parts
44 Silver wrap
45 Precipitating heavily
46 Heavenly instrument
50 Beat easily
53 Go by bike
54 La __ Opera House
56 Phase
57 Spooky
59 Land map
60 Luise Rainer role
61 Grating sound
62 Floor cleaner
63 Winter hazard

2 RADIO DAYS

by Patrick Jordan

ACROSS

1 *Love Story* author
6 Ward off
11 Lincoln son
14 "__, all ye faithful . . ."
15 Allan-__
16 Exist
17 Classic radio skit
19 Sundial numeral
20 Prairie home material
21 Head tops
22 *Poppies* artist
24 Linguist Chomsky et al.
26 With skill
27 Baryshnikov, in '74
29 Import fee
31 Blew one's stack
32 Reindeer name
33 Purpose
36 Feel sore
37 Cut into cubes
38 Hitch
39 Prepared
40 Beds of a sort
41 32 Across' owner
42 Forest clearings
44 Altered
45 *Hands __ the Table* (Lombard film)
47 Honey bunch?
48 Shoots the breeze
49 One of four for Hepburn
51 Jefferson Davis' nation: Abbr.
54 __-tac-toe
55 He spoke for Charlie
58 Actor Wallach
59 Oklahoma city
60 War-horse
61 Yahtzee cube
62 Unquestioning followers
63 Abounds (with)

DOWN

1 Lays seed
2 Canyon sound
3 Exit line for Ms. Allen
4 Mornings, briefly
5 Spotted cat
6 Balsa vehicles
7 Singer Adams
8 Course goals
9 Chicago railways
10 Big Bad Wolf's order
11 Molly's rejoinder to Fibber
12 Disney mermaid
13 Divine character
18 Reputation
23 Awry
25 Architectural double curve
26 __ Scott decision
27 Geological periods
28 Spiked club
29 Pillow casings
30 Logging-camp tools
32 Hollywood crosser
34 Stuff to the gills
35 Archaic "Oh, my!"
37 Flops
38 Coal-rich German basin
40 Low-slung hounds
41 Most meager
43 Real-estate unit
44 Cotton-tipped cleaner
45 Behaved
46 Tex-Mex dish
47 Iron or book leader
49 Stare at
50 Manuscript encl.
52 Appear
53 "No ifs, __ or buts"
56 "That was dumb of me!"
57 Short highway?

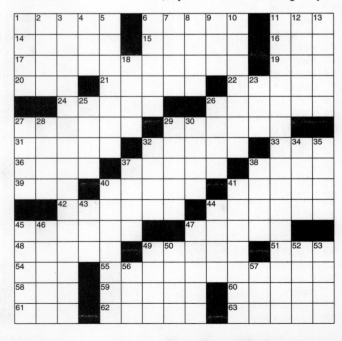

3 WOOD WORK

by Shirley Soloway

ACROSS

1 Twofold
5 Photo session
10 Plumbing problem
14 __ way (not at all)
15 Spouse of Pocahontas
16 Folklore monster
17 Car feature
19 Arizona river
20 Mythical giant
21 Prov. of Canada
22 Is wearing
23 Underwater exploratorium
25 Energy type
27 Tub
29 Other name
32 Do some stretching
37 Walk unsteadily
39 At any time
40 Actor Stacy
42 Sewing-machine inventor
43 Flavorful seed
45 Originating (from)
47 More logical
48 __ Lanka
49 Play groups
52 Grab
57 Reporter Lesley
60 Actor Stephen
62 Author Calvino
63 __ avail (useless)
64 Dolly Levi, e.g.
66 Baseball manager Felipe
67 __ *With Judy*
68 Show the way
69 Not straight
70 Seamstress Ross
71 Art Deco artist

DOWN

1 Territorial divs.
2 Loosen, as a shoe
3 Loos or Louise
4 In the neighborhood
5 Last year's jrs.
6 Santa sounds
7 Lena and Ken
8 "We're __ See the Wizard"
9 Asian holiday
10 Math exponent
11 Sponsorship
12 Woody's son
13 19th-century actor Edmund
18 Varlet
22 Angelic topper
24 Carnival employees
26 Soaps up
28 Calendar abbr.
30 *"Toujours __"* (always yours)
31 Hemmed
32 Bandleader Brown
33 Burl or Charles
34 Western elevation
35 Expand, as a business
36 __ de deux
38 __ U.S. Pat. Off.
41 Pts. of a dollar
44 Repast
46 Small amount
50 Commerce
51 Attack
53 ". . . thereby hangs __"
54 Greedy sort
55 Sport shoe feature
56 Big crowd
57 Attempt
58 Enameled metal
59 Of unknown authorship: Abbr.
61 Pretends
64 Queen of the fairies
65 "__ There" (*Pajama Game* song)

4 ANIMATED AVIARY

by Patrick Jordan

ACROSS

1 Singer Lane
5 Lincoln's in-laws
10 "Be quiet!"
14 __ *Yesterday*
15 Expect
16 Atop
17 Warners toon
19 Actress Rehan et al.
20 Pay to play
21 Like spring buds
23 Wilder or Guinness
25 Small dam
26 Having no doubt
28 Pitch __-hitter
31 Climbing plant
34 Tops
35 Sudden insight
37 Exists
38 Lantz toon
41 USPS delivery
42 Writer
43 Chops down
44 More reserved
46 123-45-6789 grp.
47 Church service
48 Limerick resident
50 Lion's home
52 Coupon clipper's need
56 Bits of grass
60 Burt's ex
61 Disney toon
63 Russian river
64 See the J.P. on the Q.T.
65 Spanish compass point
66 Count (on)
67 Drainage ditch
68 Load cargo

DOWN

1 Magician's intro?
2 Royal favor
3 Babysitter's bane
4 Won over
5 Brownish gray
6 Hold title to
7 Bohr or Borge
8 *Carpe __* (seize the day)
9 Scatter
10 Philadelphia sandwich
11 Tackles, as a project
12 Ollie's foil
13 Multitude
18 Hoyle datum
22 Variety show
24 Some fowl
26 Speak __ (make a prediction)
27 Imitative
29 Ultrabright colors
30 Painful experience
32 Ships' workers
33 That woman's
34 Leather punches
35 Reverence
36 Lifesaving initials
39 WWI battle town
40 Party pastime
45 Hands-down
47 Temperate
49 49er holdings
51 More competent
52 Speak unclearly
53 Essence
54 Actor's quest
55 Ply with flattery
57 Do a cleaning chore
58 Word form for "outer"
59 Bias, as results
62 Simian

5 FIGHTIN' WORDS

by Gerald R. Ferguson

ACROSS

1 Dear __ (columnist)
5 Fellow
9 Affix a cutting
14 *Damn Yankees* vamp
15 Polynesian dance
16 *Cosby Show* actor Hyman
17 Flapjack franchise
18 Ripening agent
19 Edmonton skater
20 Stitch
21 Disassembled
23 Striped cats
25 Roast beef au __
26 Holler
27 Risk-filled, for short
29 D.C. lobby
32 Picasso or Casals
34 Overflowing
36 City in Norway
37 U __ of the UN
38 Not fooled by
39 Post-workout activity
41 Hatfield foe
42 Cut
43 Finished
44 Yup's kin
45 Tango requirement
46 Wood basecoats
49 Attempt
54 Mathers' costar
55 Toward the back
56 "__ Me" (Roger Miller tune)
57 Wry look
58 McCarthy's trunkmate
59 Otherwise
60 Artful dodge
61 Some camcorders
62 Sight or over ender
63 "__ aside!" ("Gangway")

DOWN

1 Favored roster
2 Black tea
3 Detailed, as a description
4 Beat one's gums
5 Designer Coco
6 Sci-fi awards
7 A Baldwin brother
8 Picnic place
9 Large clam
10 Onslaughts
11 Singer Guthrie
12 Aviated
13 Petrel cousin
21 Metric measure
22 VCR button
24 Word after "look out"
27 Classic Ladd film
28 Early video game
29 Ended the work day
30 Range above tenor
31 Become tiresome
32 Deluxe
33 Arthur of tennis
34 Vandyke site
35 __ point (center of attention)
37 Scout group
40 Eight kings of England
41 Potatoes partner
44 Test pilot Chuck
45 Visibly upset
46 Perceive
47 Awaken
48 Do the floors
49 Soviet news agency
50 Cartoonist Peter
51 Sharp-witted
52 Some poems
53 Curly cabbage
57 Bride's title: Abbr.

6 LUCKY DAY

by Nancy Salomon

ACROSS

1 Emulate Bonnie Blair
6 Afrikaner
10 Co-__ (condo kin)
13 Alphabetical guide
14 Singer Lena
15 Informer
16 Achieve an upset
18 Mimic
19 Sun. talk
20 Canoer's need
21 Showy display
23 Honey
25 Comic Carvey
27 Find the mother lode
32 Packaging need
34 Actor Beatty
35 Silents actress Negri
36 Low point
37 Baby bloomer
38 Erie, for one
39 Actor Mischa
40 Posed
41 Algerian seaport
42 Win it all
46 Keep on one's __ (be alert)
47 Makes a choice
50 Drones on and on and on and on and . . .
53 Slugger Canseco
54 To the rear
56 First wife
57 Pick multiple winners
61 Midmorning
62 Eat away
63 One who volunteers, perhaps
64 Comic Carney
65 Evaluate
66 Antidrug advice

DOWN

1 Family members
2 Jabbed with a joint
3 "Not on __!" ("No way!")
4 Asian holiday
5 Blackmailer
6 Unhappy fans' cries
7 Fort __, CA
8 Pass catcher
9 Take umbrage at
10 Evangelist Roberts
11 Daddy
12 Undo a dele
14 "__ go again!"
17 Manes
22 Places for Bentleys
24 Say "Ha"
25 Title document
26 Lend a hand to
28 Coach Rockne
29 New York college
30 *The ___ of the Cave Bear*
31 Actor Holbrook
32 Word form for "bull"
33 "Zip-__-Doo-Dah"
36 Catch in the act
37 Snorts of disgust
38 Backgrounds
40 Sault __ Marie
43 Legit
44 Paladin portrayer
45 Church recess
48 Kitschy
49 All the time
50 Alpha follower
51 Start for look or see
52 Take an apartment
53 Green stone
55 Poi source
58 Lyricist Gershwin
59 Infant
60 Travel grp.

7 VEGETARIAN

by Lee Weaver

ACROSS

1 Big name in fairy tales
6 Yule poem starter
10 Edinburgh native
14 Cowboy competition
15 Beatles movie
16 Tempo
17 Ten-percenter
18 Scat queen
19 Greek war god
20 Toy weapons
23 Mouse kin
24 Many min.
25 Conclude
26 Sir Isaac's family
28 Public disturbance
30 Tavern missile
31 Sounds of glee
35 Lode load
36 Barbecue location
39 Surmounting
40 Chutzpah
43 Small opening
44 Shop tool
46 Sea, in Savoie
47 Shadowbox
48 Fruit seeds
50 Former Iranian VIP
52 Wearing away
55 "How was __ know?"
56 Pat gently
59 Vintner's need
60 MacArthur trademark
63 Arkin of *Chicago Hope*
65 Genuine
66 Chicago gridders
67 Actress Naldi
68 Icicle site
69 Ford or Pyle
70 Santa's laundry problem
71 Rural roads: Abbr.
72 Process ore

DOWN

1 Pie chart, e.g.
2 Pilot's affirmative
3 Brainstorms
4 Haberdashery department
5 May honoree
6 Eleanor's uncle
7 Shoe strip
8 Tim of *Home Improvement*
9 Let off easy
10 Whirlpool bath
11 Redhead
12 Indian or Arctic
13 Tries out
21 Burger topper
22 Make a trade
27 Ensnares
29 School semesters
31 *2001* computer
32 One thing __ time
33 Risky problem
34 Plant pest
37 Keogh relative
38 Above, poetically
41 Autos, buses, etc.
42 Muse of lyric poetry
45 Grist for DeMille
49 Night noisemaker
51 *Calvin and __* (comic strip)
52 Linda or Dale
53 Ham's equipment
54 Super-duper
56 Sawyer of TV news
57 "__ in Paris"
58 Attack
61 Church part
62 Salon offering
64 Wrestler's surface

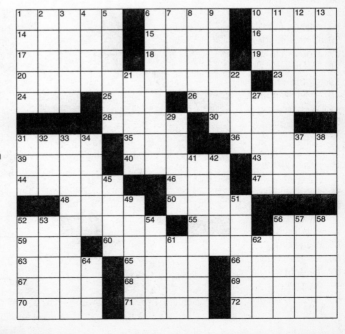

BODY LANGUAGE

by Diane C. Baldwin

ACROSS

1 Very important
6 Sunscreen number: Abbr.
9 Meal plan
13 In the know
14 Passed the word
16 Uncomfortable
17 Cut the lawn
18 Jai __
19 Uris or Spinks
20 Priestly vestment
21 Vigorous labor
24 Big birds
26 Corrode
27 Like some showers
29 Computer insert
34 Some graduate exams
35 Strong suit
36 Coffee holder
37 Erie or Huron
38 Inlets
39 Determination
40 Freezer cubes
41 Went rowing
42 Midler or Davis
43 Cargo lifters
45 Waterproof coating
46 Deer relative
47 Wall Street unit
48 Hilarious tale
53 NCAA rival
56 English noble
57 Director Kazan
58 Statement of beliefs

60 Where Moses floated
61 Force
62 Sam or Remus
63 Iditarod vehicle
64 Golf-bag item
65 Makes custard

DOWN

1 Doll word
2 Army offense
3 Hard candy
4 Mine bonanza
5 Turns in, as coupons
6 Wild guesses
7 Sport for Prince Charles
8 Imperfection

9 Use an eraser
10 Notion
11 Conceits
12 Daly of *Cagney & Lacey*
15 Abridgments
22 Put down carpeting
23 Pronged tool
25 Robust
27 Three-D
28 Vestige
29 Cote denizens
30 Angered
31 Kind of shirt
32 Old hat
33 Computer key
35 Split in the road
38 Laughed shrilly

39 Machine part
41 Certain paintings
42 Little grizzly
44 Staggered
45 "__ Loves You" (Beatles tune)
47 Sudden outburst
48 Understandings
49 Catch in the act
50 Gardner of mystery
51 Came to rest
52 Yearn (for)
54 Eric of Monty Python
55 ". . . and bells on her __"
59 Genetic factor

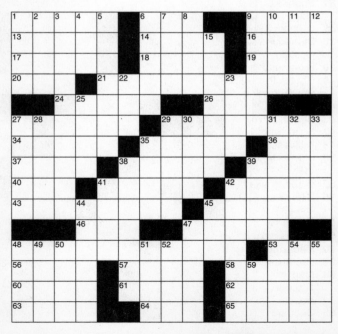

9 ALLEY OOP

by Bob Lubbers

ACROSS

1 Cinematic shark
5 Newspaper section
11 Distress letters
14 Distress words
15 Electrical unit
16 In favor of
17 Sweet treat
19 __ Tin Tin
20 Needle
21 Minimum golf score
23 Tire city
26 *Jeanne d'__*
27 Harsh breathing sound
28 Unity
30 In the center of
32 Playing-cards manufacturer
33 Painkiller
36 Work stopper
41 Radio adjuncts
42 Anger
44 Declaim
47 Facial feature
50 The Bard of __
51 Wrestlers' surface
53 Get up
54 Set free
57 Top card
58 Rock producer Brian
59 Show mercy
64 Rep.'s counterpart
65 Most certain
66 Area
67 Make an attempt
68 Trudges
69 Hazzard deputy

DOWN

1 Chore
2 "I see!"
3 Bested
4 Actress Stone
5 Swedish auto
6 Aft. times
7 Kangaroo, to a Cockney
8 Dig find
9 H.S. math subject
10 Clockmaker Thomas
11 Widen
12 Bay windows
13 Shakespearean product
18 Workday start for many
22 Singer Lopez
23 NASA affirmative
24 Understood
25 Do-fa connectors
26 Very, in music
29 *"__ bleu!"*
30 __-craftsy
31 Russian space station
34 School grp.
35 Dot of land
37 Singer Cleo
38 Investigator: Abbr.
39 Hara-__
40 Love god
43 Lea lady
44 Hardest to find
45 Plane, e.g.
46 Ant group
48 Apiece
49 Mild wind
51 Stiller's partner
52 Relevant, as an argument
55 Aide: Abbr.
56 Railroad siding
57 Legal reps.
60 Sixth sense
61 Guidry or Howard
62 Yoko __
63 __ Moines, IA

10 GEOMETRIC

by Eugene W. Sard

ACROSS

1 Australian marsupial
6 *Veni*
11 French noble
14 '50s Ford
15 Pitching great Ryan
16 Educational basics
17 Folk craft
19 Psyche part
20 Ancient France
21 German city
23 Rhode Island resort
27 Composer of *La Mer*
29 Sparta rival
30 Mideast tongue
31 Midwest airport
32 Fierce look
33 Tax org.
36 LeBlanc of *Friends*
37 Shiny fabric
38 At no cost
39 Elected pols
40 Early evening
41 Hiding place
42 Composer Gustav
44 Romantic song
45 Electricity source
47 Makes ill
48 Swiss mathematician
49 Luke Skywalker, for one
50 Prefix for center
51 Sum-thing special in arithmetic
58 Cub-scout unit
59 Representative
60 Inappropriate or excessive
61 Bishop's jurisdiction
62 Sign gases
63 Sea duck

DOWN

1 Barbie's friend
2 Lyric poem
3 Enzyme ending
4 Was ahead
5 Eaten up
6 Computer fodder
7 __ *Hand Luke*
8 Boxer né Clay
9 Game piece
10 Ugandan city
11 Opera-house section
12 Natural impulses
13 Pal
18 "Lend me your __"
22 __ generis (unique)
23 Wynonna's mom
24 Allen or Frome
25 Classic TV game show
26 Saucy
27 Plumbing outlet
28 Be entitled to
30 Change
32 Mallet kin
34 Actress Ada
35 Tournament placements
37 Auction off
38 Arkin's *In-Laws* costar
40 Union general
41 West Indian chief
43 Service winner
44 Offerings
45 *Mr. __ Goes to Town*
46 Indian currency
47 Religious groups
49 Islamic spirit
52 Era
53 Word form for "earth"
54 Verse starter?
55 Mix in
56 Regret
57 Occupational suffix

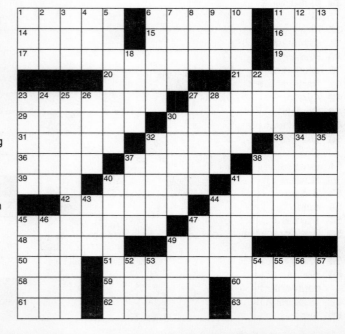

11 WEAPONRY

by Shirley Soloway

ACROSS

1 Shade of brown
6 Forbidden
10 Chatter
13 Is in first place
14 Memo abbr.
15 Hindu mentor
16 Sinclair Lewis novel
18 Author Bagnold
19 Jacqueline of *The Deep*
20 Another plate of food
22 Understand
23 Southeast Asian
25 Sluggish
26 Bar mixer
29 "My Gal __"
32 Just okay
35 Complaint
36 Trunk item
38 Eiffel's pride
40 Amtrak and B&O: Abbr.
41 Implied
42 Lyric poem
43 Pledge
45 Card game
46 Ukr., formerly
47 California jurist
50 "Let's __" (Porter tune)
52 Post- opposite
53 A Stooge
56 Workplaces
59 Anesthetics
61 Get closer to, with "on"
62 Leading forces
65 Danger
66 Riding gait
67 Banks or Ford
68 Ordinal ending
69 "Auld Lang __"
70 American Beauties, e.g.

DOWN

1 Large chunks
2 Ghostlike
3 Describe grammatically
4 Marriage vows
5 In addition
6 Highlander's hat
7 "__ was saying . . ."
8 Cave creatures
9 Supported
10 Burlap bag
11 Dry as a bone
12 Young blooms
15 School subj.
17 Sportscaster Rusty
21 Shoreline
24 *Wuthering Heights* star
26 For men and women
27 Ice block
28 Out __ (not in synch)
30 Operatic solo
31 Riga resident
32 Fr. exalted women
33 "Clumsy me!"
34 Dish from the sea
37 El __, TX
39 Memento
44 The boss, at times
48 Eniwetok events
49 Restraint
51 Sty cry
53 Wherewithal
54 Do-__ (all-out)
55 Plural makers
56 Folklore villain
57 __ accompli
58 Agile
60 Medal winner
63 Long time
64 Took nourishment

12 MEAT MARKET

by Richard Silvestri

ACROSS

1 Name in Ohio politics
5 Stand-up guy?
10 Map out
14 Concept
15 Mrs. Gorbachev
16 Swiss river
17 Opponent's program
19 Hook's henchman
20 Disseminate
21 Mine find
22 Aspen transport
23 Play the flute
25 Cross the threshold
27 Second-rank execs
29 Drenching rain
32 Woods inhabitants?
35 Everly Brothers song
37 Have a late bite
38 Penitent person
39 Garden shelter
40 Teen trauma
41 Before, to bards
42 Packing a rod
43 Puff on a pipe
44 Equivocate
46 Discharge from the RAF
48 Here's Howe!
50 Powerfully built
53 Scottish upland
55 Dance step?
57 Longing
59 Old-fashioned learning method
60 Mako kin
62 One of the Waughs
63 Barbecue leftover
64 Oklahoma city
65 Phoenician seaport
66 Lower oneself
67 Carvey or Wynter

DOWN

1 Tumbles, with "over"
2 Take for oneself
3 Word form for "iron"
4 Assume control
5 Treetop rocker
6 Dinghy adjunct
7 Joan of art
8 River to the Rhône
9 Its days are numbered
10 Prom-dress color
11 Red wine
12 Square footage
13 __-do-well
18 1990 Oscar actress Kathy
24 Derby site
26 Williams or Turner
28 Did some planting
30 Greasy thick stuff
31 Fencer's blade
32 Make stout
33 Surrounding glow
34 Yeoman of the guard
36 Matzo meal
39 Violated
40 Attacked from hiding
42 "Thrilla in Manila" victor
43 Clearheaded
45 Wool coat
47 Contemporary
49 Ignominy
51 City in Tuscany
52 Bridal sweeper
53 Army kid
54 __-poly
56 Prefix for "both"
58 Icelandic work
61 Actress Ryan

13 FIRING LINES

by Gerald R. Ferguson

ACROSS

1 Manipulated one
5 Hurry-up initials
9 Flounder stuffing, often
13 Language quirk
15 Oscar-winner as Pasteur
16 Plant no roots
17 NBA Hall-of-Famer Maravich
19 Lyric poems
20 Pick a jury
21 Parroters
23 Prop for Player
24 Big beasts, briefly
25 Where hackles are raised
28 Cereal grain
29 Utah lily
30 Merlin, for one
35 Act rashly
39 Ethical path
40 Standard
41 California fort
42 French cup
44 Agnes' *Bewitched* role
47 "Ready, __, fire!"
48 Televised faux pas
49 Germ-free
54 Stravinsky ballet
55 Indisputable evidence
57 __ Fein (IRA political arm)
58 London gallery
59 Dictation taker
60 ". . . banjo on my __"
61 Winter drifter
62 *Marie et Jeanne:* Abbr.

DOWN

1 Plumbing unit
2 Take __ view of
3 Gossamer bit
4 "__ creature was stirring . . ."
5 More than adequate
6 "A Boy Named __"
7 Foyer
8 Circular graph
9 Warble like Bing
10 Western show
11 Affirms
12 Myerson or Truman
14 Italian peak
18 Meriwether and Majors
22 Tour of duty
25 Soft drink of yore
26 Het up
27 Master Christopher's friend
29 "Hush!"
30 Instant lawn
31 Shelley's twilights
32 Greek letters
33 De Valera's land
34 Tach. reading
36 Scout bunch
37 Gump and son
38 Guy with a scope
42 South American monkey
43 Solemn assents
44 Marbles benefactor
45 Not a soul
46 Metaphysical poet
47 Out of whack
48 Lie poolside
50 Mil. grps.
51 "__ Ideas" (1951 song)
52 "*Clair de __*"
53 Son in Genesis
56 Word form for "ear"

14 PIANO FORTE

by Ann Seidel

ACROSS

1 Lofty
5 Narrow cuts
10 Listen up
14 Lot measure
15 German philosopher
16 Jessye Norman role
17 Scam
18 Love, to Luigi
19 Study all night
20 Miller or Landers
21 Largo and West
23 Let the water out of
25 JFK predecessor
26 Didn't participate
28 Religious quarters
33 Embellish
34 Spanish desserts
35 Actor Kilmer
36 Crying shame
37 North Carolina fort
38 Flowing robe
39 "__ Believer" (Monkees tune)
40 Chairs
41 Nervous
42 Canned brand
44 __ *Playing Our Song*
45 Likely
46 Arrow product
47 One on the sidelines
52 Sphere
55 Stench
56 Some spreads
57 Off base, in a way
58 Nickname for Hemingway
59 Egg-shaped
60 Trial recording
61 Hoskins role
62 Evans and Carnegie
63 Sketched

DOWN

1 Sounds of laughter
2 Revered figure
3 Bottom line
4 Put a spell on
5 Reviewer Gene
6 Auto turkey
7 Composer Stravinsky
8 Hatcher of *Lois & Clark*
9 Downhill travel of a sort
10 Computer fanatic
11 Land of Tara
12 Call it __ (quit)
13 St. Louis team
21 Goat-man
22 Fusses
24 Actor Calhoun
26 Palatable
27 Stop on __
28 Home base
29 From __ to riches
30 Academic's perch
31 Gung-ho
32 *Susan __* (Connie Stevens film)
34 Greek group
37 Rocker type
38 Layer
40 Frosh, next year
41 Humming sound
43 Actor Gordon
44 Dissertations
46 Struck down
47 Clobbers
48 Round cheese
49 "Fat chance!"
50 Thomas __ Edison
51 True-to-life
53 Vatican venue
54 What winds do
57 Tack on

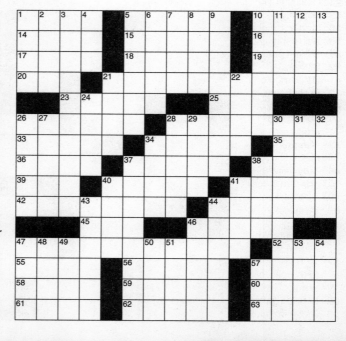

15 TO A LESSER DEGREE

by Norma Steinberg

ACROSS

1 Masticate
5 Reach across
9 Here, in Arles
12 Emanations
14 Shut
15 Negative prefix
16 Football team's option
18 Pampering, initially
19 Go by
20 Mets' stadium
21 Breadth
24 Dole's group
26 Husbands and wives
28 Magician's illusions
31 Sentry's cry
32 Skyrocket
35 Eastern European
36 Fort __, CA
37 Miserable
39 Mrs. Lennon's maiden name
40 Davis of *The Client*
42 Skillful
43 In addition
44 Start a journey
46 Dolt
48 Discount store
51 Brings up
52 Traffic components
54 Cicero, e.g.
56 Second Mrs. Sinatra
57 Inflation control plan
62 Apparatus
63 Hanks' *Apollo 13* costar
64 Comic DeGeneres
65 He served after HST
66 "Too bad!"
67 Run across

DOWN

1 Scoundrel
2 *Ben-__*
3 Pitcher's stat
4 Wac colleague
5 Feeds the pigs
6 Aplomb
7 Upward climb
8 Born: Fr.
9 Incarcerated
10 Natalie or Old King
11 Early Peruvian
13 Stages
14 Half a dance?
17 John of Monty Python
20 Recipe instruction
21 Scanty
22 Summer place for furs
23 Umpire's call
25 Part of the foot
26 Chases away
27 Auctioneer's call
29 Dorothy's home
30 Rose
33 Brewer's product
34 Musical motif
37 Weight
38 __ India (famous gem)
41 Promissory notes
43 "Now it's clear to me!"
45 Covered with blossoms
47 __ Haute, IN
49 Susan Lucci role
50 Mexican sandwiches
52 Part of a hand
53 Zealous
55 Decimal system base
57 Earl Anthony's org.
58 Leprechaun
59 Inventor Whitney
60 Buddhist sect
61 Conclude

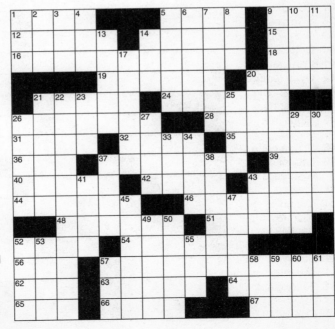

16 OASES

by Bob Lubbers

ACROSS

1 Fixed period
5 Coarse file
9 Gives (out)
14 Lotion ingredient
15 Singer Adams
16 Turn away
17 . . . in Florida?
19 Lachrymose
20 "Open __!"
21 Nebbish
23 Blue-pencil
26 Actress Susan
28 Shrill cry
31 Like some tables
33 Animal track
34 Angry
36 Ruby or Sandra
37 Competition
38 Swerves
39 Rich source
40 Gold: Sp.
41 Caravan stop
42 Oven feature
43 Less fresh
45 Mulled over
47 Helps in a crime
48 Bridge coup
49 Lauder of cosmetics
51 Braking rockets
56 "__ We Dance?"
58 . . . in Israel?
61 Desi's daughter
62 Scary giant
63 Later
64 Else

65 Actor Coward
66 Nailed a stud

DOWN

1 Emulates Gregory Hines
2 Gen. Robt. __
3 Ely and Howard
4 Butte kin
5 Ebb
6 Fuss
7 __ vous plaît
8 Moss material
9 Afternoon show
10 Turns inside out

11 . . . in Wyoming?
12 Goof
13 Eye sore
18 Arab chief
22 Desires
24 Less friendly
25 Clothing
27 Required
28 Lysander's homeland
29 . . . in Florida?
30 Fish eggs
32 Antlered animal
33 Signs of stage success: Abbr.
35 The Little Mermaid
38 Metrical writing

39 Ignited
41 Pioneer, perhaps
42 Trains, as lions
44 Howard or Uggams
46 "Roll Out the __"
50 Black
52 __ Girl ('60s sitcom)
53 "The Biggest Little City"
54 Woodwind
55 Beach surface
56 __-mo
57 Quarterback's call
59 Self
60 Before, poetically

17 SPRING FEVER

by Gerald R. Ferguson

ACROSS

1 __ in (collapsed)
6 Startling success
10 Athlete, slangily
14 Give __ berth to (avoid)
15 *Born Free* beast
16 Wrinkled fruit
17 Romantic precipice
19 Stew ingredient
20 Certain shirts
21 French physicist
23 Telegenic jurist
24 "__ clear as mud!"
25 Big parties
29 Imitative
32 __ nothing (extreme alternatives)
33 Restaurant
37 Flier's stunt
38 Darken
39 Revolutionary War general
40 Kind of drilling or shipping
42 Type of mattress
43 Consumed
44 Songbird
45 Total anew
48 Sonny's sibling
49 Gladdens
51 Enchantresses
56 Ruler before Galba
57 Attack, as a cat
59 "Help!," to Henri
60 Pittypat or Polly
61 Playwright Bernard
62 Dryer dust
63 Small band
64 To the point

DOWN

1 Young yak
2 Court-martial candidate
3 __ *Zapata!*
4 Anthony or Barbara
5 __ cri (latest fashion)
6 Casals' instrument
7 Flamenco accolades
8 Dos Passos trilogy
9 Bear with a hard bed
10 Go before "go!"
11 Double-curve moldings
12 Bow or Barton
13 Wind-powered toys
18 Tennis units
22 Failed attempt
25 Hairless
26 Spiny plant
27 Plumlike fruit
28 Got going
29 *Enoch __* (Tennyson opus)
30 Twosome
31 Doctrine
33 __ noire
34 Pro __
35 Inventor Sikorsky
36 Counting-out word
38 Cricket tool
41 Walk in water
42 Like a race winner
44 Abbr. for Clinton
45 Of the kidneys
46 Resin used as incense
47 Duelist Burr
48 __ Domingo
50 Falling-out
51 Kind of bond, for short
52 Hold sway
53 On __ with (equal to)
54 Pea holders
55 Old blade
58 __ *Town* (Wilder play)

18 WYES GUYS

by Bob Lubbers

ACROSS

1 Hard work, so to speak
6 Murray or West
9 Aristocratic
14 Poet's Muse
15 Sprite
16 Zodiac sign
17 Carved tree
18 NBA official
19 Missile housings
20 First-stringers
21 Barrymore or Merman
23 Absorbent material
27 AMEX rival
30 Chin whiskers
31 NEA member
32 Fall mo.
35 Part of BTU
36 Inter __
37 Ford or Close
39 Haul
41 Goes out of focus
42 Venice resort
43 Small shark
45 Busy insect
46 Finishes
47 Nile beetle
49 Scottish terrier
50 Melee
55 Uncouth one
57 "__ got me" ("I give up")
58 OCS grad
60 __ Mahal
63 Polish city
64 "__, I saw, . . ."
65 Lyric poem
66 Preface, for short
67 Concise
68 "It's __ the pale moon . . ."
69 Aeries

DOWN

1 Attack
2 Penned
3 Diner patron
4 "I did not think to shed __": Shak.
5 Gangster's weapon
6 Mal de __
7 Pale brew
8 Decadent
9 Poet Ogden
10 Eastern
11 Cudgel
12 Zodiac sign
13 Double curve
22 Common title starter
24 Against
25 Café au __
26 Footstool
28 English county
29 Wipe clean
32 Eyes
33 Toast sound
34 Cuddly toy
38 Pesty bugs
40 Give the alert
41 Hair holder
44 Actress Kendall
47 '60s campus org.
48 Weevil feed
51 TV honcho Arledge
52 Gives the boot
53 In the open
54 Bingo-like games
56 Suit to __
58 Ignited
59 Ade cooler
61 Tumult
62 Nozzle stream

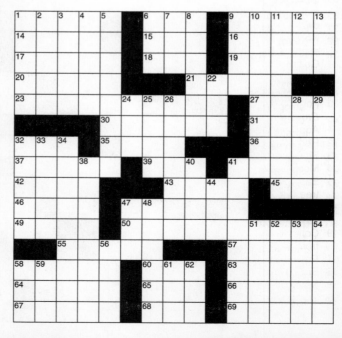

19 HALF-BAKED

by Lee Weaver

ACROSS

1 Coarse file
5 Young salmon
9 Anka or Newman
13 Commedia dell'__
14 *Kate & __*
15 Ingrid, in *Casablanca*
16 Sissies
18 Nights before
19 Musician's gift
20 Provide weapons
21 Small table on wheels
23 Forceful person
25 Wise one
26 Yuletide visitor
29 Andy of *60 Minutes*
33 Infamous motel owner
36 Norwegian explorer
38 Golfer's warning
39 Turkish title
40 Ford of *Murphy Brown*
41 Ade alternative
42 Regrets
43 Sir Guinness
44 More stable
45 East Indian fig tree
47 Knee-ankle connector
49 Comments from Sandy
51 Private Bailey
55 Biblical savior
58 Nautical yes
59 Easter meat
60 Memo notation
61 Luxurious automobile
64 Rajah's consort
65 Iroquoians
66 Hemsley sitcom
67 Salad veggie, for short
68 Understands
69 Funny Foxx

DOWN

1 Ran at Indy
2 Place in order
3 Ship's rear
4 Shooter or coat opener
5 Jack Horner's prize
6 TV alien
7 Crevices
8 Lab activity
9 "No problem"
10 Thomas __ Edison
11 PC owner
12 Shoe form
14 Kitchen cover-up
17 Half of an old singing group
22 "Long __ and Far Away"
24 Quite simple
27 Freshwater duck
28 Zodiac ram
30 Lunchtime, usually
31 Perry's creator
32 Decade tenth
33 Fishhook
34 Water, in Madrid
35 Next in time
37 Poison ivy effect
40 Trumpet flourishes
44 Curl the lip
46 *Exodus* hero
48 Bottomless chasm
50 Singer Dinah
52 Pizza-sauce herb
53 Intertwined
54 Make corrections
55 Cleopatra's beau
56 Twin to Jacob
57 Plummeted
58 Pub brews
62 Fib
63 Skiff accessory

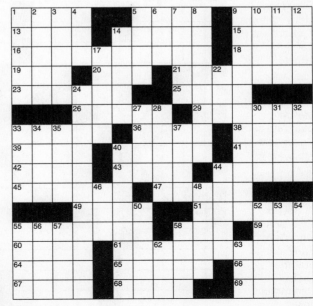

by Bob Lubbers

ACROSS

1 First year of the XVth century
5 __ avis
9 Pixieish
14 Shore bird
15 Solemn response
16 __ Haute, IN
17 Bribe money
19 Diaphanous
20 1945 conference site
22 Repair
23 Mrs. Smith's rival
26 Mystify
28 Eaten
29 Food shortage
31 Court cloaks
32 Type type
33 Mel's waitress
36 Applications
37 Band-Aid targets
38 "__ This Moment On"
39 *Mal de __*
40 Diamond data
41 Unconcerned
42 Atlas, Helios et al.
44 Sailors
45 Following
46 Annoyers
47 Taj Mahal site
48 Ingredient
51 Early strings
53 Summer cooler
57 Commercial cow
58 __ of paradise
59 Stash
60 Bristles
61 Collections
62 Muscle quality

DOWN

1 Hood and St. Helens
2 Animation unit
3 Actress Joanne
4 To the utmost
5 Went down the white water
6 Entertain
7 Rip apart
8 "__ partridge in . . ."
9 UFO pilots
10 NY governor, 1932-42
11 VCR button
12 "Goodnight __" (Leadbelly song)
13 Dweeb
18 Sinks, as a putt
21 __ *Family* (Vicki Lawrence sitcom)
23 Salk product
24 Got up
25 "Birches" poet
27 60 sec.
29 Ticonderoga and Wayne
30 Ed, Nancy, or Leon
32 Colorful horse
34 Also-ran
35 Signs
37 Ogle
38 Most level
40 *Jeanne d'Arc*, e.g.
41 Essence
43 Where *Roma* is
44 Uses cash
45 Nimble
46 Clever
47 St. crossers
49 Tennis shots
50 Canal to Buffalo
52 "__ Jane run"
54 L.A. judge
55 Scam
56 Meadow mom

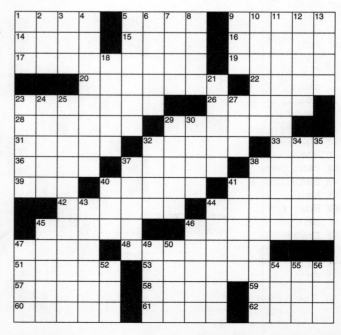

21 FABRICATIONS

by Bob Lubbers

ACROSS

1 Mutual of __
6 NBA officials
10 Donaldson of ABC News
13 Falana and Albright
14 "I __ Song Coming On"
15 Arafat's grp.
16 Acts
17 Cancel
18 Football filler
19 '40s jump tune
22 Nile snake
25 Tipplers
26 Party-game animal
27 First-rate
29 Endowment source
30 Harlem nightspot
33 Indian princess
37 One who carries
38 Dearie
39 Hayes or Reddy
40 Short drive
41 Bail out
43 Farm yield
45 Bargain sign
46 More crafty
49 Boa, e.g.
51 Isr. neighbor
52 Dreamt
55 Fuss
56 Lofty lobbies
57 Effrontery
61 Scout Carson
62 Street violence

63 Couric of *Today*
64 Nav. rank
65 Indulge, with "on"
66 Aft end

DOWN

1 Aged
2 A Stooge
3 Pub quaff
4 Muslim pilgrimage
5 Rater
6 Auberjonois and Russo
7 Counting-out word
8 Baloney
9 Wild West oasis
10 Give a hand?
11 Wonderland visitor
12 Comic Amsterdam
14 Skip meals
20 Colorful horse
21 Disrobe
22 Savings and checking: Abbr.
23 Sailing vessel
24 Page of music
28 Letterer's aid
29 Candid cameraman
31 Poker item
32 Parcel
34 Assumed name
35 Nice __

36 Cartoonist's helper
39 Nags
41 Author Alger
42 Gray frost
44 Esteem
46 Conscious
47 *The Thinker* sculptor
48 Honks
49 Wheat alternative
50 Stephen and Gardner
53 Fox __ (dance)
54 "Egad!"
58 Western Indian
59 Knight's title
60 Mid-morning

22 RETURN TO SENDER

by Gerald R. Ferguson

ACROSS

1 Gooey globule
5 Culinary mavens
10 Rude kid
14 Othello's tormentor
15 "Sweet __ O'Grady"
16 Not on tape
17 Capital on a fjord
18 Appliance maker
19 Congregational response
20 Brother of Ham
21 Be oneself again
23 D.C. edifice
25 Costa del __, Spain
26 Stung
30 Sphere of action
34 Tibetan priests
35 "Phooey!"
38 Bone __ (study)
40 Infamous Idi
41 Aboveboard
42 Identification
43 Airfoil, e.g.
44 "__ all night" (store sign)
45 Actress Moorehead
46 Rose-colored dye
48 Side by side
50 __ Aviv
52 P.O. course
53 Agassi offering
59 Quite the style
63 Anne Nichols' hero
64 Lake near Donner Pass
65 Courtroom ritual
66 For fear that
67 Keep clear of
68 Mother of Zeus
69 Graph lines
70 Musical pauses
71 Clammy

DOWN

1 Life stories, for short
2 Whip end
3 Give the glad eye
4 Backfires
5 Flash Gordon portrayer Buster
6 __ erectus (early man)
7 Biblical barterer
8 Natives of Vaasa
9 Land bordering the Pacific
10 Talk out of turn
11 Terza __ (verse form)
12 With: Fr.
13 Race dist.
22 Freddy's street
24 Rockies and Catskills: Abbr.
26 Popular side order
27 '50s First Lady
28 __ acid (organic compound)
29 Tiresome one
31 Elastic strap
32 Crest alternative
33 Mighty volumes
36 Duffer's dream
37 Sister of Nancy and Frank, Jr.
39 Empty __ (Mulligan sitcom)
41 Texas' symbol
45 Lund or Fleming
47 Conglomerate inits.
49 AKC classifications
51 Go
53 ". . . to be jolly, __ . . ."
54 Goat with curved horns
55 Shine's companion
56 Hardens
57 PPP
58 Sporting-equipment name
60 "Yuk-yuk"
61 Agenda part
62 Old boy

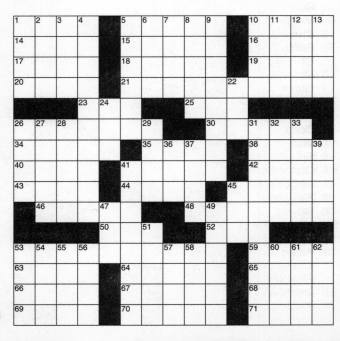

23 HOUSEWORK

by Bob Lubbers

ACROSS

1 ERA, e.g.
5 Awful movie
9 Selects
14 Actress Negri
15 Reverend Roberts
16 Little bird
17 Lou Gehrig's nickname
19 Teeny-__
20 Fruit-and-nut candy
21 *Candid* __
23 Estuary
25 Special abilities
28 Calmly
33 Lowest minor league
34 Occupied
35 Shoestrings
37 Guitarist Montgomery
38 Chore
39 Rob and Chad
40 Obtains
41 Quantity: Abbr.
42 Hemmed, perhaps
43 Dodger Pee Wee
44 Spurn
46 Dismantled tents
48 Ski runs
50 Daystar
51 Life's work
53 Lassos
58 Adam of *Chicago Hope*
60 Cover up
62 Play unit
63 Congers
64 New York canal
65 Overfilled
66 Depend (on)
67 Blocker and Rather

DOWN

1 Twirl
2 *Corrida* charger
3 Felipe of baseball
4 Sharp flavor
5 Baby shoe
6 Bruin great
7 Fem. opposite
8 Sheepish cry
9 Eleanor and Jane
10 "If __ Carpenter"
11 Sports wipeout
12 Barbie's beau
13 Hog wallow
18 Author Bret
22 Spiked clubs
24 Permit
26 Feared fly
27 Talked back to
28 Instruments for Shankar
29 Shiny paint
30 Book's cover
31 Inquire
32 Went off-course
36 Yields
39 "__ Entertain You"
40 Precious stone
42 Derided
43 Princess of India
45 *Seinfeld* role
47 Barbie's bow
49 Underground duct
52 Former South Korean president Syngman
54 Transfixed
55 O'Hara mansion
56 A __ "apple"
57 __ *Gotta Have It* (Spike Lee film)
58 Buffoon
59 Co. founded by Sarnoff
61 Unwell

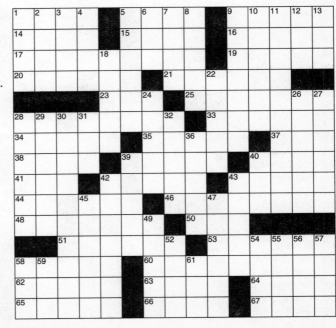

24 GO WEST

. . . .

by Dean Niles

ACROSS

1. __ 1 (the speed of sound)
5. Covers snugly
10. Zig end
13. She loved Narcissus
14. Harriet's husband
15. "Take __ your leader"
16. Streetcar
17. Ross or Rigg
18. __ *Three Lives*
19. Tranquil
21. Corrective
23. Old Greek coin
25. Really sore
26. Site of the Alhambra
29. Start of *Hamlet*
31. For fear that
32. Cuban dance
34. Blossomed
38. "Zounds!" is one
39. __ box (TV)
40. Burrow
41. French cheese
42. Grassland
43. Road charge
44. Felt sorrow over
46. Brought to office
48. Coffee choice
51. Blood-component word form
52. Pecuniary
56. Miming a crow
60. Dross
61. Missouri River city
63. Élan
64. Singer Smith
65. Pedestrian
66. Meal for Mr. Ed
67. Blvds.
68. Reek
69. Slangy affirmative

DOWN

1. New York team
2. Farmland division
3. Singe
4. Traditional tune
5. Beverly Hills address
6. Submachine gun
7. Corporate VIP
8. Cows, old-style
9. Junction
10. Woody Allen film
11. "I Cried __" (LaVern Baker song)
12. Pious
15. Voight/Hoffman film
20. Hoops org.
22. Break a fast
24. Extolled
26. Whipped-cream measure
27. Bring up
28. __ spumante
29. Where we live
30. Open audition
33. Wire width
35. Plant anchor
36. Fashion mag
37. Fuse metal
45. Flying cigar, e.g.
47. Time period
48. Office furniture
49. Showy display
50. Winter wear
53. Rowdy groups
54. Mosque priest
55. Sugar source
57. *"Dies __"*
58. Actress Naldi
59. "How about that!"
62. *2001* computer

25 METALLURGY

by Lee Weaver

ACROSS

1 Sly look
5 Have a snack
10 Clarinet relative
14 At rest
15 Musical drama
16 Ship's jail
17 Military medal
19 Tart taste
20 Movie ad
21 British business abbr.
22 Issues an invitation
23 Riveter of note
25 Towel inscription
26 Rim
30 Stir-fry pan
31 Chanted prayer
34 Simba's relatives
36 Sired
38 Have the flu
39 Absent with permission
41 Use over again
43 Word form for "foot"
44 Explorer Polo
46 Backpacker, e.g.
47 Phonograph inventor
49 IRS month
51 Attention-getter
52 Airport info
53 Soak, as tea
55 Sardonic response
57 Ave. crossers
58 Medium's medium

63 Like Clinton's office
64 Southern snake
66 Football arena
67 Be of use
68 Saharan
69 Possesses
70 Stair post
71 Like Ichabod Crane

DOWN

1 Tilt, as a ship
2 Singer Adams
3 Scat-singing queen
4 Guns the engine
5 Rob of *Quiz Show*
6 Package delivery org.

7 Resembling mesh
8 Packing box
9 Inflexible
10 Acquire
11 Essentials
12 Farm sound
13 Hen's outlay
18 Poetic adverb
24 Serious
25 Sub door
26 Run away to marry
27 Supped in style
28 *Private Benjamin* star
29 Compass pt.
31 West of Hollywood
32 Makes angry

33 Paying attention
35 Mead's study site
37 Feel one's way
40 Family vehicle
42 Songwriter Harburg
45 Tool
48 Stable areas
50 Vend again
53 Kitchen cooker
54 Each
55 King of the road
56 State firmly
57 Read quickly
59 Melville captain
60 Pianist Peter
61 Eve's oldest
62 Whirlpool
65 Dessert choice

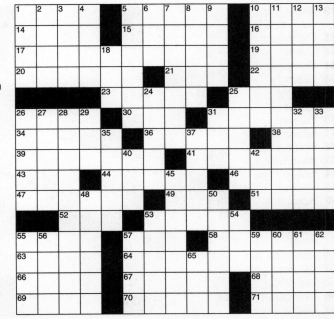

26 SHORT SUBJECTS

by Bob Lubbers

ACROSS

1 Sign gas
5 Packaged paper
9 This could be a stretch!
13 Raison d'__
14 5-sided
16 Small fellow
18 Trespassers, in a way
19 __-mo
20 Conducted
23 Krazy __
24 Attempts
26 Gusted
28 Feudal farmers
32 Wind up
33 Garfield or Garner
35 Kukla's pal
37 Small fellow
42 *Muy __* (very good)
43 Carter and Gwyn
45 Composer's deg.
47 Solemn words
50 Famed surrealist
51 Live's partner
53 Alias indicator
55 "King" Cole
56 __ *Were King*
57 Adolescent
62 Small fellow
67 Hunts for data
68 Rabbit cousin
69 *¿Cómo __ usted?*
70 Competed
71 Seer's vision

DOWN

1 Unused
2 Summer, in Paris
3 Mined matter
4 Speaker Gingrich
5 Tell
6 Actress Markey
7 Suit to __
8 Bryn __, PA
9 Chaney or Nol
10 Signs on the dotted line
11 Posted
12 Butter subs
14 Court bargains
15 General idea
17 Vex
20 He preceded RMN
21 Airline to Israel
22 Bruce's ex
25 Went tottering
27 Den installation
29 Automaton
30 Waitress at Mel's
31 Like a fox
34 R-V fillers
36 __ Saud
38 Gorcey or Durocher
39 Movie deer
40 __ Bator
41 Actress Joyce of *Roc*
44 Pose
45 Stands up to
46 Small-town sign: Abbr.
48 Extreme dislike
49 Antarctic birds
51 British "quart"
52 Actress Talbot
54 Paintings and sculpture
58 U.S. missile
59 First year of the 22nd century
60 Yearn
61 Reverberation
63 Vote for
64 Emoter
65 Anger
66 Score for Retton

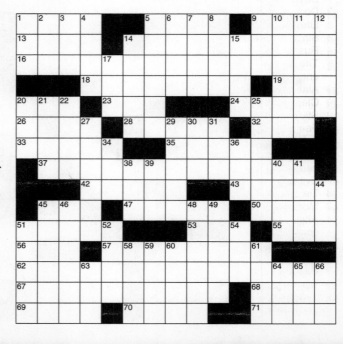

27 WATER COLORS

by Elizabeth C. Gorski

ACROSS

1 Sugar source
5 Hairdresser's need
9 Ol' Blue __ (Sinatra)
13 Computer language
14 Killer whale
15 Ward of *Sisters*
16 1984 Prince film
18 Family group
19 Direct path
20 "Love __ Simple Thing"
22 Inc., in England
23 Beach souvenir
25 Angel toppers
27 Dove call
28 Donkey call
30 Life: Ger.
33 Singer Lovett
34 Russian ruler
37 The whole enchilada
38 Alan or Kathy
39 Clean-air org.
40 Sticky stuff
42 Feel sore
43 Bunch of bees
45 Namesake, perhaps
47 Evil laugh
48 Tie again
50 More grimy
54 Altar constellation
55 Musical sense
57 Faint light
59 Baseball great Willie
61 1981 Fonda film locale

63 Pour __ (try hard)
64 Author Wiesel
65 French heads
66 Essence
67 Noticed
68 Smelters' materials

DOWN

1 Hints
2 Concur (with)
3 "There's __ like home"
4 *Invisible Man* author Ralph
5 Jazzman Chick
6 "Are you a man __ mouse?"
7 Cato's 1102
8 Wailing spirits
9 Computer key
10 China-Korea separator
11 Make happy
12 __ of Iwo Jima
13 Police call: Abbr.
17 Word form for "within"
21 Satisfied sound
24 Musical beats
26 Longitude opposite: Abbr.
29 Gen. Robt. __
30 Be a slowpoke
31 House add-on
32 1977 Linda Ronstadt song
33 Like some curtains
35 Tax mo.
36 Aries
38 First-aid kit contents
41 Center starter
43 Mounted, as a stone
44 Plaintive cry
46 Unified
47 Donut feature
48 Harold of *SCTV*
49 Muse of poetry
51 Nash of poetry
52 Overact
53 Philosopher Descartes et al.
56 Acting job
58 Hwys.
60 NBC show since 1975
62 Prevaricate

28 EQUITATION

by Gerald R. Ferguson

ACROSS

1 Truman opponent
6 Pant
10 Right-angle shape
13 Earthy color
14 Church platform
16 Day, to Dolores
17 Dilutes
18 Gaucho's rope
19 *Platoon* setting
20 Guzzler
21 1917 tune, with "The"
24 Spooky
26 Bill's companion
27 Close by
29 Cliburn, e.g.
33 Snapshot
34 Doughboys
35 Balloon filler
37 Misreckons
38 Swiss capital
39 Arsenal stock
40 Brillo rival
41 John Barth's ___ Goat-Boy
42 More morose
43 Happens to
45 Servant's garb
46 Latin I word
47 Actor George
48 Mail service of 1860
53 Stars and Bars initials
56 Sundial number
57 Attach (to)
58 Cries of derision
60 Set a price
61 Relents, with "up"
62 Hardy's nickname
63 Service charge
64 Newshound's need?
65 Aquarium favorite

DOWN

1 Ellipsis elements
2 Yodeler's playback
3 Yukon Territory capital
4 Direction ender
5 "Make up your mind!"
6 Avant-___
7 "Shake ___!"
8 Leading player
9 Infant's game
10 Author Ferber
11 Fact twister
12 Weak, as an excuse
15 Some synthetic fabrics
22 Cover
23 Me, to Mimi
25 Consumes
27 Acts like
28 Pulsate
29 Peels
30 Quaint hotels
31 Revolver inventor
32 Microwave feature
34 Holler
36 Actor Calhoun
38 Jeff Davis, in the 1880s
39 Part of T.A.E.
41 Specialized cell
42 Top banana
44 Actress Wray
45 Guitarist Paul
47 Rationality
48 Chanteuse Edith
49 Belgian river
50 Reebok competitor
51 100 centavos
52 Old World stags
54 Move a little
55 Sailing
59 Flamenco accolade

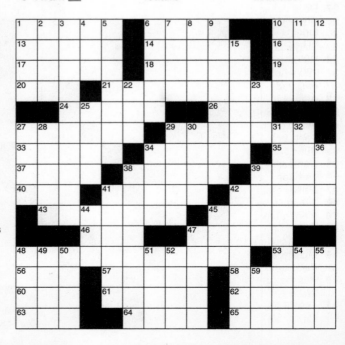

29 TIME SHARING

by Bob Lubbers

ACROSS

1 Accord
5 Food thickener
9 Pie nut
14 Actor Jannings
15 Arizona city
16 Make amends
17 Lillian Hellman play
20 Pigpen
21 Ambiance
22 Thumbed (through)
23 Legal penalty
24 R.I. neighbor
25 Declare
28 In awe
29 Poetic dusk
32 Arise
33 Hunters' prey
34 Rights org.
35 Leroy Anderson tune, with "The"
38 Comic Johnson
39 Son of Eve
40 *Kate & __*
41 Cow comment
42 Mr. Rogers
43 Goes over the limit
44 Twitches
45 Sailor's greeting
46 Singer Nina
49 Brio
50 Beatnik's home
53 Slim-waisted shape
56 One at __ (individually)
57 Jane's dog
58 Prayer end
59 Challenger
60 Short trips
61 Tiff

DOWN

1 Church seating
2 "I __ my wits' end!"
3 Metropolis
4 RN's offering
5 Quantity
6 Art style
7 Nick and Nora's pooch
8 Stadium sound
9 Mom or Dad
10 Allen or Frome
11 Stylist's forte
12 Charles' sister
13 Require
18 See 11 Down
19 Ran off to wed
23 Pasture divider
24 Dromedary
25 State of India
26 Prefix for foam
27 __ Domingo
28 Evaluated
29 French school
30 Spanish hero
31 Uses the microwave
33 Comic Kaplan et al.
34 Bowler's site
36 Package
37 Golfer Donna
42 Identify, slangily
43 Elevator passageways
44 Singer Mel
45 Columnist Joseph
46 Roe source
47 Smidgen
48 American naturalist
49 Phil of hockey, familiarly
50 Bailer's tool
51 Zone
52 Small amount of progress
54 Ember dust
55 Car fuel

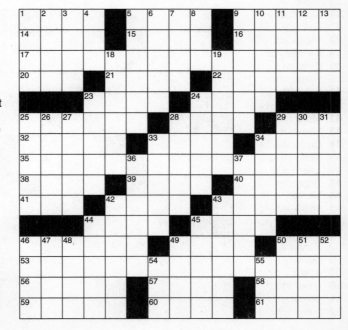

30 FRUCTIFEROUS

· ·

by Gregory E. Paul

ACROSS

1 Dance unit
5 Doone's love
9 Singer Khan
14 Trim
15 Incense output
16 Person
17 Austen's Woodhouse
18 Belafonte song "locale"
20 Cochise, e.g.
22 "Amo, __, I love a lass"
23 Sault __ Marie
24 Bacon portions
26 Regarding
28 Solti's stick
30 Brightly colored shawl
34 Separately
37 Moniker
39 "I've Got __ in Kalamazoo"
40 Director Wertmuller
41 Enjoy the taste of
42 Fishing gear
43 Short jacket
44 Drain section
45 See eye to eye
46 Taper
48 Mantel
50 26 fortnights plus
52 Bedroom furniture
56 Horned viper
59 Love god
61 Discerning
62 Firecracker

65 "No man __ island"
66 Marsh bird
67 Pianist Gilels
68 Matador's need
69 Papal bull, e.g.
70 Gainsay
71 Leg joint

DOWN

1 Harpoon
2 Cigar city
3 Bombeck et al.
4 After-dinner drink
5 Rules of Order guy
6 Crete peak
7 Spanish woman
8 Inge forte
9 Pure
10 Airline transfer point
11 Freeman Gosden role
12 Pitcher Jim
13 Poker stake
19 Sadat's predecessor
21 Preliminary race
25 Sub's tracker
27 Manicurist's device
29 Maritime
31 "Ain't She Sweet" songwriter
32 Cracker spread
33 Otherwise
34 Kim's husband

35 Gyro bread
36 Before long
38 Scooter
41 R-rated, perhaps
45 Ice and Iron
47 Memorized
49 In a lackluster way
51 Clothed
53 Singer Anton
54 Military encampment
55 Actress Taylor
56 Aspirin target
57 Molt
58 Beautiful girl
60 *Picket Fences* town
63 Fox sitcom
64 Andy Gump's wife

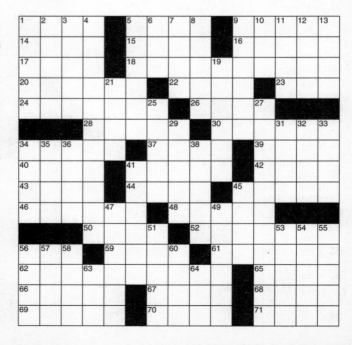

31 PIGGY BANK

by Gregory E. Paul

ACROSS

1 Postal codes
5 Davis or Standish
10 "Memory" musical
14 Sch. on the Rio Grande
15 *Let's Make __*
16 What George couldn't tell
17 Singer Horne
18 Needle
19 National League quorum
20 Footed vase
21 Midship area
23 Not mine
25 Shows (the way)
26 Jolson tune
28 Horseman's mount
30 Nervous
31 Rich Little, e.g.
32 Cheese city
36 Skillfulness
37 Most meddling
40 "__ no idea" ("Who knows?")
41 Reviewer Rex
43 Grassland
44 Fess up
46 Mattel rival
48 *Fawlty Towers* star
49 Merchant
52 Prickler
53 Kid-TV channel
56 Out of tune
59 Double curve
60 Hersey bell town
61 Diabolic
62 Ghostly sound
63 Barcelona boys
64 Russian river
65 Coastal birds
66 Plow man
67 Bunch

DOWN

1 Radio-alphabet ender
2 Seneca's street
3 Small-time
4 Hot tub
5 Adult
6 Schemes
7 Sitcom producer Norman
8 Sunrise direction
9 Certain train cars
10 Voltaire novel
11 Green-card holder
12 Colored
13 Tracks down
21 Anne or Mary
22 Fish delicacy
24 Switch positions
26 Cowboys' emblem
27 Existed
28 Upset
29 Prepared to drive
31 Riding the waves
33 Ned Buntline work
34 Alamo rival
35 Apportion
38 __ Park, KS
39 Claw
42 *Oliver Twist* author
45 German article
47 Actress Ruby
48 Select
49 Folklore creature
50 Austerity
51 Indian, for one
52 Corelli or Domingo
54 Garfield's pal
55 Jutlander
57 NBA quorum
58 Blemish
61 Nav. rank

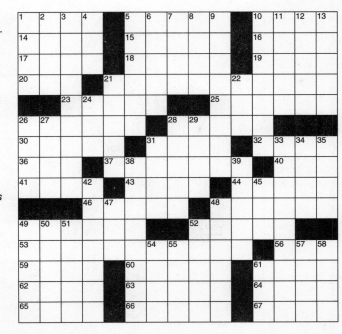

32 THE ENVELOPE, PLEASE
by Gerald R. Ferguson

ACROSS

1 Ridiculed
6 Health farms
10 Funny one
14 Bolt together?
15 Prepare dinner
16 Matty or Felipe of baseball
17 Kind of boom
18 Green Gables girl
19 Shipshape
20 It requires a signature
23 Ice-cream portion
24 Time period
25 Horse rope
29 Bears witness (to)
33 Bread spread
34 City on the Allegheny
35 __ tree (stuck)
37 Vocalized message
41 CPR expert
42 Permanent location?
43 Pro's opposite
44 Tuxedo accessories
46 Acted autocratic
48 The lot
49 It. island
50 '62 tune
59 Istanbul native
60 "Yes __?"
61 Bright signs
62 Racer Luyendyk
63 Contort
64 "See the point?"
65 Sow's mate
66 Louis and Carrie
67 Tiffs

DOWN

1 Pianist Dame Myra
2 Out of kilter
3 ZIP code's predecessor
4 Grand-scale
5 Agree (on)
6 Sell tickets illegally
7 Watering hole
8 Top-of-the-line
9 Bony
10 Jib material
11 Nautical term
12 Hearty laugh
13 Import tax
21 Football filler
22 Dunne or Papas
25 Gardener's need
26 Out on __ (at risk)
27 Slow, in music
28 Get dressed, with "out"
29 Countertenors
30 High schooler
31 Rotations
32 Outpouring
34 Stare at
36 In the course of
38 Basketry fiber
39 Establish conclusively
40 Chevron offering
45 Pedestrian
46 "Fie!"
47 Primates, for short
49 Organ parts
50 Brief effort
51 Continental prefix
52 *Rigoletto* rendition
53 Fay of *King Kong*
54 Regarding
55 Don't sell
56 Kappa preceder
57 Fit of anger
58 Jet-setters' jets

33 ATTACHMENTS

by Bob Lubbers

ACROSS

1 Ocean
4 Old hat
9 Anecdotes
14 Picnic pest
15 E.T., e.g.
16 Combat zone
17 "Am __ understand that . . ."
18 Lost color
19 Zoo structures
20 Long-necked bird
23 Morning hrs.
24 Necks of the woods
25 Clark or Rogers
26 Ascot
27 Tree home
28 Took a risk
31 Mooring
32 Plane starter
33 Oppose openly
34 Emergency device
38 "__ Day's Night"
40 Eisenhower and Turner
41 Penny
42 Add-on
44 Info
48 __-Magnon man
49 One: Fr.
50 Western elevations
51 Poet's "above"
52 Kids' game
56 Condition
58 Gossip fodder
59 Ring cheer
60 Indonesian island
61 Arab chief
62 Ely or Howard
63 Confidence games
64 Fop
65 Hesitant syllables

DOWN

1 Pacific island
2 Complete
3 Makes amends
4 Mamas' mates
5 Jai __
6 Threshold
7 Planter's purchase
8 Stand the test of time
9 Crass
10 Coach Parseghian
11 Diplomatic staff
12 Foes
13 Back-talkers
21 Tit for __
22 How some pkgs. arrive
28 "Agnus __"
29 Circle segment
30 Batman's sidekick
31 Major leaguer
32 Also
33 Dollar fractions: Abbr.
34 Broad view
35 School class
36 Guitar relative
37 Ritter or Beneke
38 Greets rudely
39 Dissenter
42 Landers or Reinking
43 Approached
44 Morning condensation
45 On land
46 Clothes alterer
47 Poplars
49 Computer owners
50 Cheerful
53 Cougar
54 Federal agents
55 Tilled
57 Male turkey

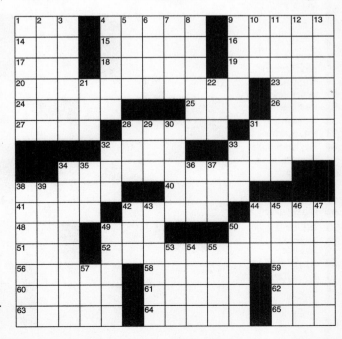

34 ON LOCATION

by Dean Niles

ACROSS

1 *Six Degrees of Separation* playwright
6 Wrapper
10 Swedish actress Andersson
14 Expropriate
15 Walesa, e.g.
16 Above, in Berlin
17 Postal unit
18 __ about (around)
19 A.G. Janet
20 What the pendulum swung over
21 Garrison Keillor location
24 __-pitch softball
25 Gold or silver
26 Lyricist Gershwin
27 Robert Waller location
34 __ away (passed pleasantly)
36 Subtracting
37 Want-ad initials
38 Unclear
39 Ginseng relative
40 Taj Mahal site
41 Part of 49 Across
42 Comfort
44 Author Norman
46 MacKinlay Kantor location
49 Marker
50 Novel ending
51 No.-cruncher
54 Grace Metalious location

59 Leading
60 Operation Overlord beach
61 Finish off
62 SWAT team actions
64 Symbol of recalcitrance
65 __ out (supplemented)
66 *Sesame Street* character
67 Water extension
68 Halting colors
69 Dancers painter

DOWN

1 Catches breath
2 Up to
3 Dissected
4 "What's the Frequency, Kenneth" group
5 Blast off
6 Big wheels have them
7 Top-drawer
8 Torpid
9 Large gestures, e.g.
10 The B in FBI
11 "__ to differ"
12 "Let there __ mistake"
13 Golf club
22 Soulless
23 Warner __
28 __ Khan
29 Times bygone
30 New beginning
31 Passing over
32 Ripped up

33 1066 or 1492
34 "Hold it, Trigger!"
35 Goldie of the screen
39 R&R site
40 Feel feverish
42 Switch ending
43 To shreds
44 This 'n' that
45 Transmogrified
47 __-or proposition
48 Delicacies
52 Where conductors stand
53 Church recesses
54 Water server
55 Needle case
56 New Haven school
57 Jab
58 Schubert song
63 Exist

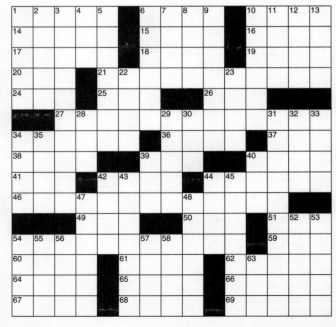

35 MEAT MARKET

by Lee Weaver

ACROSS

1 Falls (behind)
5 Black Sea port
11 Outlaw
14 Neutral color
15 Gasped
16 *All About __*
17 Small change
19 Poetic eternity
20 Word link
21 On the __ (fleeing)
22 Bushy hairdo
23 Mountainous nation
25 Bullring cheer
26 Calf catcher
30 CD-__ drive (computer adjunct)
31 Beach hut
34 Overhead
36 Future flowers
38 "You're it" game
39 Confuse
41 Ancient Greek warship
43 Inquire
44 Statue of Liberty prop
46 Alarm sound
47 Data summary
49 Director Spike
51 Attention getter
52 Slippery, perhaps
53 Type of lily
55 Help a felon
57 Sushi sauce
58 Monet or Rubens
63 Scrooge's comment
64 Old-style side whiskers
66 Bikini part
67 Narrated anew
68 Spin like __
69 Summer hrs. in Delaware
70 Easels, e.g.
71 Makes lace

DOWN

1 Nobelist Walesa
2 "__ Breaky Heart"
3 Clutch
4 Of that kind
5 First game
6 Newsman Rather
7 Kindle
8 Rob
9 Appear to be
10 Say more
11 Tower of London guards
12 Declare positively
13 Pianist Peter
18 Barbie's beau
22 Priest's vestment
24 Tough question
25 Desert refuge
26 *M*A*S*H* clerk
27 Too big
28 Soft, flat-crowned topper
29 Actress Gabor
31 Naval rank: Abbr.
32 Designates
33 Representative
35 Index listing
37 Lucy's sidekick
40 Earned
42 Tear
45 Lone Ranger portrayer Moore
48 Halloween mo.
50 African antelopes
53 Terra __
54 Trajectory path
55 Singer Lane
56 Shakespearean epithet
57 Lard kin
59 Not this
60 Small amount
61 Dalmatian's name
62 Cookbook abbr.
64 __ *Doubtfire*
65 Antiquated

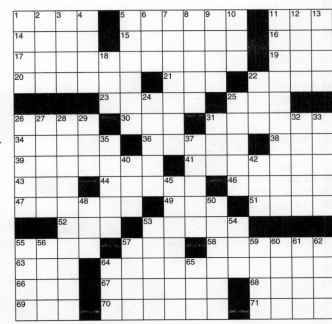

by Bob Lubbers

ACROSS

1 Old hat
6 Singer Brooks
11 Health resort
14 Ski resort
15 Hawaiian "hi"
16 Tic-__-toe
17 Stylish home feature
20 Take on
21 Architect, e.g.
22 Mr. Onassis
23 "__ was saying . . ."
24 Prepares flour
28 Attack
30 Docile
34 __ five (rest)
35 Numero __
37 Kin
39 Thicke film of '92
41 Belgian capital
43 Mess up
44 Homer's kid
45 Regimen
47 Global specks
51 Sociologist Hite
53 __ Khan
55 Model Carol
56 Copy
60 __-European
61 Path to success
65 Vast vessel
66 Oven gadget
67 Reagan appointee
68 Sound of disapproval
69 Double curves
70 Roles

DOWN

1 Titled Turks
2 Seek, with "after"
3 Morale
4 Dry
5 *Bambi* aunt
6 Like Victorian houses
7 Canadian prov.
8 Colorful horse
9 Wispy
10 Rabbit relatives
11 RR depot
12 __ de deux
13 High card
18 '60s records
19 Beasts, so to speak
23 Baxter and Rice
25 Not swarthy
26 Ring win: Abbr.
27 D.C. VIP
29 Exceed
31 Got up
32 *A Few Good* __
33 Threat ender
36 Newspaper page
38 Lofty lobbies
39 Certain
40 1051, to Caesar
41 Kid's ammo
42 Stadium sound
46 Spuds
48 Plane, at trip's end
49 Firstborn
50 Stashes
52 Overact
54 Toothpaste type
57 Eye part
58 Flat hats
59 Suit to __
60 Brainstorm
61 Urban transport
62 Spanish gold
63 *King Kong* studio
64 Elec. unit

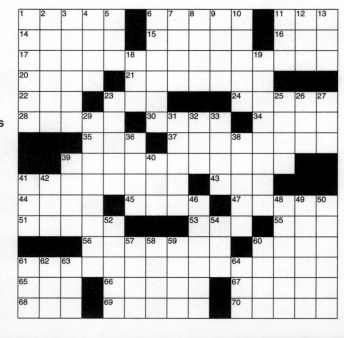

37 TRAIN RIDE

by Bob Lubbers

ACROSS

1 Olympian Paavo
6 Take __ (travel)
11 GI address
14 Ryan or Tatum
15 Hunt goddess
16 Statesman Hammarskjöld
17 House covering
19 __ Abner
20 "__ boy!"
21 Afternoon parties
22 Missouri tribe
24 Haberdashery items
26 Hair band
30 "Bali __"
31 Comic singer Sherman
32 Cad
35 Light fog
39 Boxer's move
42 Word form for "huge"
43 Pot base
44 Mongolian mountains
45 Posed
47 G-man Ness et al.
48 Kind of knife
54 Jewelry weight
55 Indian princess
56 Backtalk
60 Ripen
61 Some LPs
64 Author Deighton
65 Tube descriptor
66 Own up
67 Before, poetically
68 Rope loop
69 Encounters

DOWN

1 Exploding star
2 Part of BTU
3 Lease
4 Yucatán Indians
5 Ailing
6 Arles aloha
7 Word before wave or basin
8 Mrs. Gorbachev
9 Lodging place
10 Chinese temple
11 Governor Stevenson
12 Pitcher Satchel
13 Leers at
18 Greek portico
23 Reaction provokers
24 Discover
25 Syngman of Korea
26 Raise crops
27 Hand-lotion additive
28 Fake coin
29 Rummy game
32 Reagan or Howard
33 Unconscious
34 Employ
36 A fan of
37 "Vamoose!"
38 The one here
40 "What __ God wrought?"
41 Ashen
46 Joins the cast of
47 Blue-pencil
48 Minimum wage
49 Bet
50 Dunne or Papas
51 Psychologist Bettelheim
52 Bowling alleys
53 Conductor Previn
56 "Smooth Operator" singer
57 Top
58 Revue bit
59 JFK arrivals
62 Yoko __
63 St. Louis gridder

38 SHOW OF HANDS

by Gerald R. Ferguson

ACROSS

1 Grassy plain of Argentina
6 Towel word
10 "Phooey!"
14 Forcefully
15 Genesis name
16 Skip over
17 Shabby
18 Arizona Amerind
19 NYC art center
20 High-tech defense initials
21 Billy Joel, e.g.
24 Bumblers
26 15 Across, to Eve
27 A sorry bunch?
28 Abyssinia, today
33 Bad to the extreme
34 *Gigi* star
35 Cuba, e.g.: Abbr.
36 Sponsorship
37 Tear up
38 Word form for "eight"
39 Traffic behemoth
40 Dickens title start
41 Tarsal joint
42 Pioneers
44 Cherry, e.g.
45 Above, to Keats
46 1923 loser to Dempsey
47 Baseball award
52 Mainframe brain: Abbr.
55 Miffed
56 Mideast carrier
57 Benefits
59 Embossed emblem
60 Auctioneer's last word
61 Yonder
62 Gloria's TV pal
63 "Terrible" age
64 Completely satisfied

DOWN

1 Tablets
2 In the course of
3 Nails expert
4 Greedy one
5 "__ in a storm"
6 Belly laughs
7 Black, in poesy
8 Bank takeover?
9 Sloppy
10 Pizza cheese
11 Chinese island seaport
12 Fourth dimension
13 Lead player
22 Freudian concerns
23 T-bone's locale
25 Subtraction word
27 Rascal
28 Noble chaps
29 Shade source
30 Urban crook
31 Basketry fiber
32 Popular houseplant
33 Entanglements
34 Burn slightly
37 Most stringent
38 "Movin' __" (*The Jeffersons* theme)
40 Skipper's word
41 Runs in
43 Walk unsteadily
44 Arith. process
46 Throws in one's cards
47 Lillian or Dorothy
48 Creme-filled cookie
49 Adjective for 1996
50 Aura
51 French composer
53 French papa
54 Pre-owned
58 "That's it!"

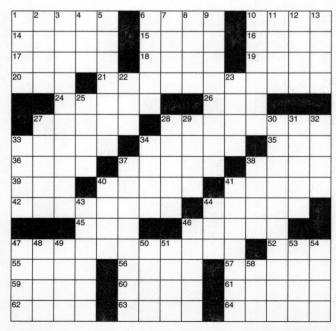

39 UP IN THE AIR

by Diane C. Baldwin

ACROSS

1 Enthralled
5 Spanish houses
10 Winter vehicle
14 Hodgepodge
15 "Remember the __"
16 Garr or Hatcher
17 Ripening agent
18 California county
19 Gloomy forecast
20 Pocket-watch feature
22 Fencing sword
23 Dole's group
24 School assignment
26 Challenges
29 ". . . a __ every purpose under heaven"
32 Army officer
35 British noblewomen
37 Feel poorly
38 Musical work
39 Groucho prop
40 Canadian Indian
41 Sleep activity: Abbr.
42 Word before space or limits
43 Cowboy gear
44 __ de corps
46 "Shoo!"
48 Spicy sauce
50 Foist (on)
54 Guinness or Baldwin
56 Safety-deposit sites
59 Drench
60 As __ (generally)
61 Louver
62 Feed the kitty
63 Telegraph operator
64 Ireland
65 Nuisance
66 Certain joints
67 Fortuneteller

DOWN

1 Strays
2 Pond plants
3 __ the sky (illusory hope)
4 Twisters
5 RV
6 Winglike
7 Agra attire
8 Chemical compound
9 Glee-club member
10 Small river
11 1996 and 2000
12 Part of HOMES
13 Enjoy a banquet
21 Play the lead
25 __ boom bah
27 Prepare to publish
28 Wise ones
30 Neckwear
31 Bread spread
32 Extra
33 Zoo favorites
34 Checker-cab items
36 Artist Chagall
39 Trims
40 University areas
42 Olive product
43 Tibetan monk
45 Clamor
47 TV talker Joan
49 Brother of Moses
51 Hardy's nickname
52 Stunned reaction
53 Fragrant compound
54 Quickly, briefly
55 __ Star State (Texas)
57 Stocking shade
58 Swiss painter

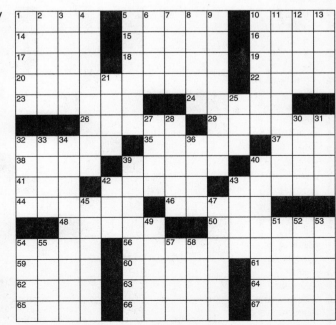

by Bob Lubbers

ACROSS

1 Fancy dance
5 Soda-shop order
9 Mends
14 Gen. Robert __
15 Garfield's nemesis
16 Some collars
17 Moola
19 Fire: Ger.
20 4:00 china
21 __ 17 (Holden film)
23 A Bobbsey twin
25 Hid
28 Blabbered
33 Campout cook's can
34 Rave-review excerpt
35 Gay __
37 Bachelor's last words
38 "A __ plan . . ."
39 TV reporter Shriver
40 Norse god
41 Rile
42 Parts
43 Alla __ (musical direction)
44 Required
46 Avers
48 Kind of bass
50 Sp. lady
51 Mark of *St. Elsewhere*
53 Manor
58 Tolerate
60 Diaper catch
62 Auctions, e.g.
63 HoJo rival
64 Tear
65 Desert trees
66 Badgers
67 Keats works

DOWN

1 Waist cincher
2 Lotion additive
3 Melodious Horne
4 Diamond's moniker
5 Hod load
6 Summer drink
7 Reclines
8 Circus structures
9 Let the air out of
10 Relaxed
11 One of Teddy's troopers
12 Compass dir.
13 Lith., once
18 Playwright Jean
22 Befuddled
24 Himalayan kingdom
26 Salad veggie
27 Lorna's kin
28 Street urchins
29 Turkish inn
30 1775 battle
31 Eagles' grp.
32 Challenged
36 Stands up
39 Computer adjunct
40 Mouths: Lat.
42 Keep down
43 Detonation
45 Royal headband
47 Obnoxious ones
49 Contents of a hand-drying bag
52 Okinawa capital
54 Novice
55 Imitated
56 Fork part
57 Finishes
58 Nile cobra
59 Sheepish remark
61 Traffic hazard

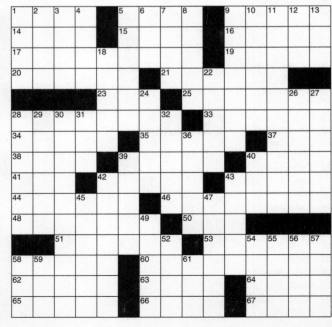

41 OVEN-FRESH

by Bob Lubbers

ACROSS

1 Very short putt
6 LL.B. holders
10 Train unit
13 Korean, e.g.
14 Chart
16 '20s auto
17 Wise one
19 Coach Parseghian
20 "Wait __ the sun shines . . ."
21 Domain: Abbr.
22 Spanish hero El __
23 From Libya, perhaps
27 Second film versions
29 Life story, for short
30 Time periods
32 One of two teams
33 __ *Well That Ends Well*
35 Biblical garden spot
37 __ firma
40 Boxing prop
41 Against the clock
43 Open a little
44 Top floor, maybe
46 Latvian capital
47 Alight
48 Arabian sultanate
50 Manor worker
52 Corp. boss
53 Like some shirts
56 Skater Hans
58 Append
59 Scull needs
61 Three __ match
62 Actress West
63 Wage earner
68 Nav. rank
69 Barrel slat
70 Oak fruit
71 Korean soldier
72 Portent
73 Ancient instruments

DOWN

1 Auto fuel
2 Doctrine
3 Actress Farrow
4 Cuban patriot José
5 Lure
6 In the past
7 Horse's gait
8 Customer
9 Church tops
10 A-one
11 Lofty lair
12 Auto paths
15 Recluse
18 Red wine
23 Addis __
24 Boned fish
25 Nostalgic furniture
26 Low point
28 *Let's Make* __
31 Big trucks
34 *Ghostbusters* goo
36 Mideast desert
38 Indian princess
39 Passion
42 Scopes' attorney
45 Chocolate substitutes
49 Close by
51 Lampshade ornament
53 More docile
54 Hersey town
55 Night vision?
57 Sinatra or Reagan
60 Store (up)
64 Hideaway
65 "Neither rain __ snow . . ."
66 Before, poetically
67 TLC providers

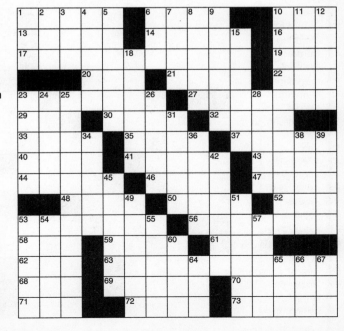

42 UP A TREE

by Gregory E. Paul

ACROSS

1 Actor Baldwin
5 Senate staffer
9 Summarize
14 PBS program
15 Pub pints
16 *Aïda*, e.g.
17 Give off
18 Envy, pride, etc.
19 Nasser's successor
20 *Little House* town
23 Actor Vigoda
24 Make up (for)
25 "Believe __ not!"
27 Coddle
30 Sony rival
33 Oklahoma city
34 Dark fur
37 Pale
38 Lassie's offspring
40 Former women's magazine
42 Camping need
43 Everything, to Ernst
45 Viper
47 *"Sprechen __ Deutsch?"*
48 Pittsburgh gridder
50 Country singer Tex
52 Health clubs
53 __ Carta
55 Ron of *Tarzan*
57 Howard Hughes' flying boat
62 Singer Vaughan
64 __ mater
65 Footnote abbr.
66 Entertain
67 High schooler
68 A few
69 Berth option
70 Helper: Abbr.
71 Chicken chow __

DOWN

1 Freshly
2 __ Linda, CA
3 Devilish
4 Forty winks
5 Rustic
6 Straighten
7 Art category
8 Exxon, formerly
9 __ stone (famous inscribed slab)
10 Fed. ecology group
11 Fragrant box
12 Arafat, for one
13 Top of the head
21 Western Indians
22 Seneca's seven
26 Hops kiln
27 Actress Irene
28 Grownup
29 Vermont product
30 Grazing group
31 Skater Sonja
32 Prefix for mural
35 Stock pessimist
36 Little shaver
39 Ooze
41 Pepper or York
44 Horror-film heavy
46 Dempsey's domain
49 Sixth sense: Abbr.
51 Chinese religion
53 Stubborn ones
54 Summits
55 Rebekah's son
56 Genie's abode
58 Pro __ (proportionately)
59 Orchestra reed
60 __ Valley, CA
61 Actress Barbara
63 Peer Gynt's mother

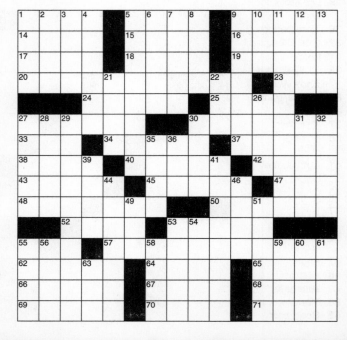

ACROSS

1 Medicinal amount
5 Irving hero
9 Gridder Brian's kin
14 Admired one
15 Vicinity
16 Exchange
17 Nick's mate
18 "__ Be Cruel"
19 Clinton defense secretary
20 Senior activist
23 Wind up
24 Catch
25 Pete of tennis
27 McMurtry's __ *Dove*
32 Fragment
33 Imitate
34 Shoe material
36 Cacophony
39 __ Valley, CA
41 Babel structure
43 ". . . and children of all __!"
44 Kind of shoes
46 Metal strands
48 Dine
49 Choral voice
51 Chopin work
53 Stress
56 A: Ger.
57 Building add-on
58 Wonderland grinner
64 Move furtively
66 Hgt.
67 Part of T.A.E.
68 Sierra __
69 Scale starters
70 Caught in the act
71 Lou Grant portrayer
72 Diary capacity
73 Andrew's dukedom

DOWN

1 Doorbell sound
2 Aroma
3 Marsh bird
4 Comic Boosler
5 Wanderer
6 Elvis __ Presley
7 Monthly payment
8 Walkways
9 Jeff Bridges film
10 Apr. payee
11 Deceptively weak one
12 Minneapolis suburb
13 Transmits
21 Refuse to bid
22 "The Raven" monogram
26 Malay outrigger
27 Eye protector
28 Mayberry moppet
29 Victim of Hercules' first labor
30 Feline sound
31 Newsman Newman
35 Finnish architect Saarinen
37 O'Casey or Penn
38 Villa d'__
40 Troubles
42 Phone piece
45 Decal
47 Recipe direction
50 Aah's partner
52 On pins and needles
53 Inventor Nikola
54 French pronoun
55 Hard up
59 Gin flavor
60 Greek Juno
61 Singer Laine
62 Affirm
63 Army vehicle
65 Compass dir.

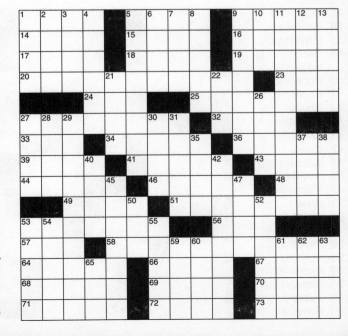

44 MS. PRESIDENT

by Lee Weaver

ACROSS

1 Raced
5 Former Iranian ruler
9 Sax range
13 Cod and Hatteras
15 Nero's robe
16 Prejudice
17 Tropical spot
18 Bring up
19 Poet Pound
20 *Designing Women* star
23 Dress (up)
24 Sushi sauce
25 Actor Wallach
26 Dubai, e.g.
28 Bowler's targets
30 Remain
31 Mongolian desert
35 Quagmire
36 Goose egg
39 Yemen port
40 Search, in a way
43 Fly like an eagle
44 Do a double take
46 Way off
47 Goofs
48 Atmosphere
50 __ *Here to Eternity*
52 Wine holders
55 Santa __ winds
56 Big fuss
59 Burning
60 *Charlie's Angels* star
63 Pallid
65 Rescue
66 Some beneficiaries
67 Swing around
68 Ukraine capital
69 '50s tune, e.g.
70 Sea swallow
71 Part of A.D.
72 Annoyance

DOWN

1 Oodles
2 Place to lounge
3 Industrial glue
4 Salami emporium
5 Kitchen device
6 Gardener, at times
7 Playing marble
8 Seraglios
9 Tad's dad
10 Cleopatra to Burton's Antony
11 Seer's deck
12 Inedible orange
14 Snooze
21 *Cheers* mailman
22 Paris hotel
27 Poker ploy
29 Show disdain
31 Needlefish
32 Lyric poem
33 One of *The Golden Girls*
34 Become liable for
37 Elevator compartment
38 Many mins.
41 Bosnian city
42 Monetary unit of Iceland
45 Expedition
49 "Seward's Folly"
51 He-manly
52 Wild party
53 Pews divider
54 Washday worry
56 Stage whisper
57 Day or Duke
58 Beginning
61 Tied up
62 Kind of seaweed
64 Hankering

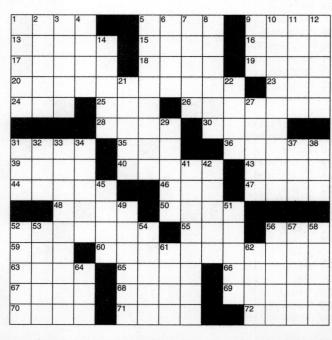

45 ON THE GRIDIRON

by Bob Lubbers

ACROSS

1 Cotton variety
5 Nearly all
9 Obligations
14 Eye part
15 Blues singer James
16 *Kate & __*
17 Angler's carryall
19 Actress Massey
20 Afternoon china
21 Greek dialect
23 I love: Lat.
25 Remain loyal to
28 Grows severe
33 Indian tent
34 Interest gouging
35 Farm buildings
37 Hole piercer
38 Coal boxes
39 Hoagies
40 Russian river
41 D.C. summer setting
42 Gluts
43 __ nous
44 Repair a shoe
46 Arrayed, as for battle
48 Dreaded flies
50 "My Gal __"
51 Actor Omar
53 Redeems, with "in"
58 '30s bandleader Jones
60 Motorcycle actuator
62 Witchlike woman
63 Possess
64 Opera solo
65 Elias and Julia
66 Agitate
67 Yin and __

DOWN

1 *12 Monkeys* costar
2 *"Dies __"*
3 Shiny mineral
4 Inquires
5 __ in St. Louis
6 Pony-players' place: Abbr.
7 Ancient colonnade
8 Levies
9 Some newspapers
10 __ Islands (former name of Tuvalu)
11 Street celebration
12 Can metal
13 Vast expanse
18 WWII admiral
22 Kruger and Preminger
24 Beginning
26 Take warning
27 Hollered
28 Lyndon's veep
29 Stage whispers
30 Be boss
31 Jrs., next year
32 Begat
36 Finishes last
39 Healthier
40 One, to Pedro
42 Oil sources
43 Fitzgerald et al.
45 Fuel gas
47 Green Bay player
49 Sect of India
52 Decree
54 Remain
55 __ kiri
56 Actress Moran
57 Male deer
58 *"__ bin ein Berliner"*
59 Broadway hit sign: Abbr.
61 106, to Nero

46 UNREAL ZOOLOGY

by Patrick Jordan

ACROSS

1. Indian honcho
6. Fracas
11. Barker and Bell
14. Calgary iceman
15. Talk-show host Hamilton
16. Benevolent brother
17. Toni Tennille's partner
19. Slugger's stat
20. Overly formal
21. __ in (collapsed)
23. Brief raids
27. Alleges
29. Preparing to drive
30. __ T. Washington
31. Asian ape
32. Not as good
33. Potsdam pronoun
36. Abounding (with)
37. Mingles
38. '60s hairstyle
39. Slangy agreement
40. Penalized a speeder
41. Stereo systems, for short
42. Stockpiles
44. Clothes hater
45. Life's little jokes
47. Bemoans
48. Translucent
49. Verdi opera
50. Actor Chaney
51. Howling deejay
58. Amin of Uganda
59. Torch's crime
60. Numbers game
61. Peace, to Petrarch
62. Letter closing
63. Long time

DOWN

1. Postal abbr.
2. Miss. neighbor
3. Preserves preserver
4. Grant of gospel
5. Dinner portion
6. Indian wraps
7. __ up (stay quiet)
8. Joplin tune
9. Pitch __-hitter
10. Flapjack
11. Game-show magnate
12. *Seascape* playwright
13. Slides on ice
18. Small remnant
22. Exist
23. Tale
24. Eagle's nest
25. *SpaceCamp* actor
26. Toe the __ (obey)
27. Hollowed apples
28. One of Ben's boys
30. Takes on Tyson
32. *The __ of War*
34. Critic Judith
35. Multitudes
37. Deep mud
38. Assistant
40. Approach to the green
41. Word preceding "possible"
43. Undivided
44. Nothing, in slang
45. Long Island town
46. Role for Valerie
47. Describes precisely
49. Get an __ effort
52. Coronado quest
53. Baton Rouge inst.
54. Regular guy
55. One __ time (singly)
56. Midpt.
57. Puts flat on the canvas

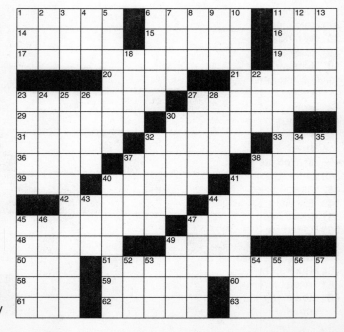

47 BREAD BOXES

by Lee Weaver

ACROSS

1 Bread spread
5 Hillside, to Burns
9 Desist
13 Field of study
14 "He's __ the coop!"
15 Fill the hold
16 Be a couch potato
18 Presser's need
19 Printer's measures
20 Learning method
21 Movie awards
23 Ringed planet
25 Mall madness
27 Country walkway
29 Flabbergast
33 Like a cirrus cloud
36 Realty unit
38 *Herr*'s mate
39 Not doing much
40 Pigtail
41 Deposited, as eggs
42 Machine part
43 Pulls a heist
44 Breathers for fish
45 Small bag
47 50%
49 Enjoys a book
51 Itsy-bitsy
55 Quantity
58 Wahine's dance
60 Black cuckoo
61 Arrests
62 Walking-race style

65 Horse's gait
66 Linda of *Dynasty*
67 Pianist Hines
68 Matches a raise
69 __ avis
70 Ran in the wash

DOWN

1 Drake and gander
2 Bakery output
3 Bakery input
4 Lout
5 Ink mishap
6 Libertines
7 Wheat beard
8 Gave approval to
9 Ad vignette
10 O'Hara home
11 Scent
12 Corrals
14 Façade
17 Deck out
22 Complete collection
24 Socially prominent classes
26 County, in Louisiana
28 Stassen or Lloyd
30 Russian river
31 Hammer's target
32 Ineffectual bombs
33 Hairpieces
34 Mind find
35 Blinds part
37 Urban vehicle
40 Rest between exertions
44 Collect slowly
46 Egg layer
48 Map book
50 Harvest wool
52 Dating from birth
53 Night noise
54 Intersection sign
55 Picnic pests
56 Colt's mom
57 Double-reed instrument
59 Forearm bone
63 Gabor or Perón
64 Young lady in society

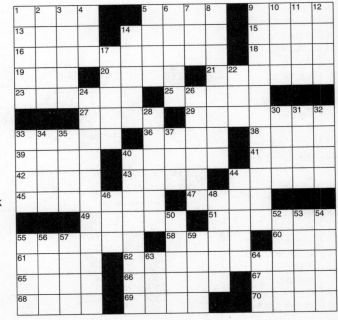

by Bob Lubbers

ACROSS

1 Acting jobs
6 Sales pitch
11 Actor Torn
14 Soap __ (TV fare)
15 Sculpt
16 '70s ring champ
17 Broadway production of 1933
19 Ailing
20 Make believe
21 *Inter* __ (among other things)
22 Sailor's "yes"
25 Yalie
26 Moving aimlessly
28 Frying medium
30 Bridge seat
33 Bandleader Shaw
34 Gripping tool
36 Romantic isle
38 Broadway production of 1994
43 Show scorn
44 Lawrence's turf
45 Carried
48 Challenge
50 Calm
51 Disinclined
53 Atty.'s degree
55 Golfer's prop
56 Breath freshener
57 Bitty bug
61 Part of Q&A
62 Broadway production of 1929
66 Brenda or Peggy
67 Pay the tab
68 Praise
69 Curved letter
70 Shouts
71 Personal log

DOWN

1 Kitchen vessel
2 GI address
3 Confederate soldier
4 Ensnare
5 "__ bleu!"
6 Nova __
7 Peel
8 De-pleat?
9 Circumvent
10 Guided
11 Scold
12 Urbana footballers
13 Pontius __
18 Actress Holm
21 O'Hare posting
22 European range
23 North Korean border river
24 Ireland
27 More scarce
29 Sweet dish
31 Cross the goal line
32 Greek consonant
35 Tears apart
37 Little drama
39 Flower area
40 Border (on)
41 Irk
42 Evans or Carnegie
45 Chili roll
46 Sheep
47 Tightens (up)
49 Armadas
52 __ nous
54 Rode Greyhound
58 Russian city
59 Notary's need
60 1111, to Caesar
62 Pig's digs
63 Greek vowel
64 Neither's partner
65 Tarzan portrayer Ron

49 BEJEWELED

by Bob Lubbers

ACROSS

1 Alan of *Shane*
5 Knocks on a door
9 Candle centers
14 Kampuchea's continent
15 Singer Adams
16 Global speck
17 Haberdashery department
18 Verse
19 A+, for one
20 Circular stain
23 An NCO
24 Gardner of mysteries
25 Runs off (with)
27 Buffalo NHLers
30 From scratch
32 __ Jima
33 Required
35 Science rooms
38 Did stitchery
40 Toddler
41 Coin of the realm
42 At rest
43 Procession
45 Blocker or Rather
46 Shoe part
48 "__ Fideles"
50 Rectories
52 Issue forth
53 H.S. math subject
54 Where manners are taught
60 Steam
62 Clare Boothe __
63 __ mater
64 Author Zola
65 Biblical brother
66 Tide type
67 Opus for nine
68 Recognizes
69 Eternities

DOWN

1 Mary's pet
2 On a cruise
3 Force
4 Dancer's yokemate
5 Beat back
6 Pueblo material
7 Marina sight
8 Trucker's rig
9 Shimmy
10 Neighbor of Syr.
11 Greet, in a way
12 Small anchor
13 Leaves in, editorially
21 Vogue
22 Dweeb
26 Norway's capital
27 Emphatic Spanish assent
28 Wowed
29 Alley target
30 Revere
31 Greek cheese
34 List ender, for short
36 Trounce
37 "Auld Lang __"
39 Poet's nighttimes
41 Corpsman
43 Elegant
44 Maidens
47 Hush-hush
49 Fuel type
50 Expert
51 San Antonio landmark
52 TV host
55 "Oh, dear!"
56 Cartoonist Goldberg
57 Margarine
58 Arabian gulf
59 Race segments
61 Bullring cheer

50 SPORTING CHANCE

by Gregory E. Paul

ACROSS

1 Impudence
5 Primitive
10 Q-Tip, e.g.
14 London gallery
15 Fire-truck rolls
16 Charter
17 Kind of vaccine
18 Occurrence
19 Radiate
20 Baseball event
23 "Phooey!"
24 Registers
25 Lithium, e.g.
27 Dispatch funds
30 Self-effacing
33 Young woman
36 Parched
38 Car accessory
39 Tempe sch.
40 Enliven
42 Frequently, to a poet
43 Flutist
45 Location
46 Chip in a chip
47 Solid alcohol
49 Actor Alain
51 Provide with new troops
53 Inventor Otis
57 Catch
59 Yachting prize
62 Clarinet cousin
64 Patti LuPone role
65 Corn spikes
66 First name in politics
67 Peter and Franco
68 *Glamour* rival
69 Stewpot
70 Italian city
71 "Those Were the __"

DOWN

1 Vermont resort
2 Composer Copland
3 Begin
4 Clouseau portrayer
5 Bishop, for one
6 Meander
7 __-friendly
8 Jeans material
9 Regard
10 That girl
11 Tennis event
12 Sills solo
13 Playwright Henley
21 Dr. of rap
22 Shop
26 Nabokov novel
28 Spring flower
29 Sheepish
31 Prepare flour
32 Schlep
33 Glove-box items
34 "__ bigger than a breadbox?"
35 NFL event
37 Palm fruit
40 Odor
41 Put on the air
44 Poetic palindrome
46 Ouzo flavoring
48 Bewail
50 Slangy suffix
52 Diehard's cry
54 La __ (Milan landmark)
55 __-burly
56 Church nooks
57 It's forbidden
58 Genesis name
60 Laugh: Fr.
61 "Blame __ the Bossa Nova"
63 Greek vowel

51 WESTERN OMELET

by Bob Lubbers

ACROSS

1 Light ray
5 Wrestling needs
9 Emily and Wiley
14 Taj Mahal locale
15 Latin I word
16 Bizarre
17 Precipitation
18 Nerve
19 Wood finish
20 Western advanceman
23 Hood's weapon
24 Actress Gardner et al.
25 Lee of *Baywatch*
27 Hound dog
30 Cavort
32 "__ live and breathe!"
33 Retrieve, as a trout
35 Labor
38 Vetoes
40 __-tac-toe
41 Desist
42 Vane direction
43 *Remington* __
45 100 yrs.
46 More sacred
48 Gibson of tennis
50 Musically unkeyed
52 Brainstorm
53 Also
54 Western footwear
60 __ nous
62 Ranch helper
63 Flapjack franchise letters

64 Guide the wheel
65 Caruso solo
66 Word form for "China"
67 Wrongful acts
68 Waiter's load
69 Nearly all

DOWN

1 Italian seaport
2 Actor Richard
3 Dry as a desert
4 Crazes
5 Tycoon
6 Pile up
7 Powder base
8 Normandy battle site
9 Part of USPS
10 Not at home
11 Western vehicle
12 Test
13 Actress Berger
21 States
22 Atop
26 Microscopic bug
27 Curse
28 Largest continent
29 Western weapon
30 Airman
31 Paddy crop
34 Diminutive suffix
36 "Oh, that's what you mean!"
37 Horne or Olin
39 British school
41 VIP, for short
43 Missile housing
44 Billie Holiday's sobriquet
47 They tie shoes
49 Lao-tzu's teachings
50 Alamogordo event
51 Lone Ranger's sidekick
52 Ancient Greek region
55 Exclamation of disbelief
56 Roseanne's former surname
57 Buckeye State
58 Oodles
59 Dick and Jane's dog
61 On a pension: Abbr.

52 GROUP THERAPY

by Norma Steinberg

ACROSS
1 Film spy Matt
5 Merchandise
10 Animal lovers' org.
14 Mayberry moppet
15 Tolerate
16 Plane or rasp
17 Prejudice
18 Desi's daughter
19 Football linemen
20 Step into the strike zone
23 Menageries
24 Wallach and Whitney
25 Under
28 D'Artagnan ally
31 Jai __
32 Something seen
34 Polynesian finger food
37 Create a defense
40 Used to own
41 Goes in
42 Model Macpherson
43 Conductor's prop
44 In the wink of __
45 Consequently
47 Hosiery shade
49 Annual bash
55 Mini-lake
56 *Atlantic City* director
57 "Up, up and __!"
59 *Picnic* playwright
60 Hunter constellation
61 Leslie Caron film
62 Garden site
63 Easel
64 Pace

DOWN
1 Prefix for goblin
2 Of grand scope
3 Perjurer
4 Era of the dinosaurs
5 Ralph __ Emerson
6 Lies adjacent to
7 Like some desserts
8 Adams or Brickell
9 Ooze
10 Filches
11 Loren's husband
12 Encryptions
13 Pacino and Capp
21 "Awesome!"
22 Hotelier Helmsley
25 *Goldberg Variations* composer
26 Director Kazan
27 Frying substance
28 Pale
29 Section of seats
30 "__ the family?"
32 Jacket opening
33 "Sock __ me!"
34 Gdansk native
35 Just
36 Words of understanding
38 Fewest
39 Top brass
43 Weight
44 Oklahoma city
45 Investor's choice
46 Door pivot
47 Synthetic fiber
48 Invert
50 Managed-care grps.
51 Small missile
52 *Inter* __
53 Simpleton
54 New Haven campus
55 Dessert option
58 Lyricist Harburg

53 SUITS ME

by Rich Norris

ACROSS

1 Charity
5 Not secret
10 Brother of Cain
14 Golfers' props
15 More ashen
16 Cartoonist Walker
17 Playing field
20 Nav. rank
21 Greenish blue
22 Snow bits
23 Fr. holy woman
24 Show remorse
25 France's Mont __
26 Until now
28 "Anything __" (Porter tune)
29 Cut (off)
32 Annoys
34 Enveloping glow
35 Scrooge, e.g.
38 Summer in France
39 Nudge
40 Pathway
41 Rust causer
43 Total
44 H.S. juniors' exam
45 More than enough
49 Hurler Warren
51 Prefix for gram or dermis
52 Suffix for press
53 Load the trunk again
55 Ardor
56 Greek letters
57 Joseph Conrad story
60 Earth: Ger.
61 Walkway material

62 Johnson of *Laugh-In*
63 Pro votes
64 Actress Veronica
65 Hopalong Cassidy portrayer

DOWN

1 Optimally
2 Makeshift shed
3 Goofed (up)
4 Wind dir.
5 Becomes murky
6 Deem important
7 Singer Fitzgerald
8 Eric the __
9 Toys (with)

10 Capital of Jordan
11 Mail-order company
12 Sea eagle
13 Old Ford models
18 Trade
19 Word of woe
25 Not interested
27 Imitated
28 "Understand?"
30 Gold, to Pizarro
31 Fido's foot
33 Lone Star State denizen
34 Old one, in Germany
35 __ *Doubtfire*
36 Marker, for short

37 *The Maltese Falcon* detective
39 Connect, as a chain
41 Wisconsin city
42 Clothes
44 Agreement
46 __ uno
47 Reliable
48 Agreed with
50 Trims the excess
51 Make joyful
53 Actress Perlman
54 Weird
55 Mild cheese
58 Ft. Myers' home
59 Catch, as a felon

ACROSS

1 Taj Mahal site
5 Roe source
9 Upstart
14 Buck Rogers' mentor, Dr. __
15 Relief org.
16 Harden
17 Zone
18 "Too bad!"
19 Edgar __ Poe
20 Wild West showman
23 Hallucinogenic initials
24 European range
25 Yens
27 Do __ (fight)
30 Mexican state
32 French assent
33 Assert
35 Dresden's river
38 Long-limbed
40 Televise
41 Amber, e.g.
42 Butter substitute
43 Moolah
45 Inventor Whitney
46 Turn in
48 Complied with
50 Quarterback Len
52 Bettor's words
53 Classic car
54 Legendary deejay
60 Ascended
62 Jai __
63 Siouan speaker

64 Che's amigo
65 Ink a contract
66 Harvard rival
67 Trials
68 Fencer's sword
69 It's simple

DOWN

1 *Pequod* captain
2 Spiritual leader
3 Atoll barrier
4 PLO chief
5 Surgeon's tool
6 Auras
7 Part of U.A.R.
8 Lucie's dad
9 Theater district

10 Blow up, as a photo: Abbr.
11 WWII admiral
12 Delete
13 __ an ear (listens)
21 Calm
22 Queue
26 Canadian Indian
27 Western tie
28 Fantasy writer Jean
29 1994 Amateur Golfer of the Year
30 Paris divider
31 Monster
34 Den
36 Inclination to anger

37 Oklahoma town
39 Hits the road
41 Spring harbinger
43 Pebbles' pet
44 Lettuce type
47 Dries (off)
49 Delights in
50 Beer category
51 High home
52 Reflection
55 Emit coherent light
56 Toss
57 __ impasse (stuck)
58 Soft drink
59 Retain
61 Collection

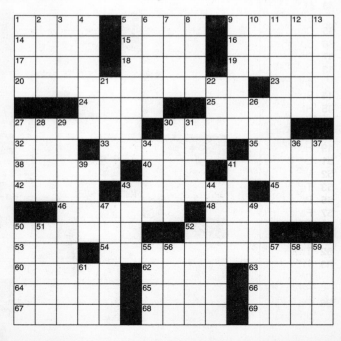

by Fred Piscop

ACROSS

1 Covenants
6 Talk like Daffy Duck
10 Party bowlfuls
14 G sharp's alias
15 Director Preminger
16 Singer Guthrie
17 Location
18 Toasty
19 Sweetheart
20 Hallucinations of a sort
23 Arm art
25 Simile center
26 Suburban add-on
27 __ *Town* (Wilder play)
28 Ghost
31 Bad habits
33 *Mmes.*, in Spain
35 Comics cry
36 Spongy ground
37 Doctor's pledge
43 Cuttlefish's defense
44 Buddy
45 Hair maintenance
46 Packing unit
49 Holy book
51 L-P connectors
52 Males
53 Totally
55 Puts forth
57 Far from the truth
61 Salt, chemically
62 Thug
63 The __ Kid (Western hero)
66 Pack (in) tightly
67 Tennis situation
68 Spud
69 Writer Ferber
70 Strong alkalis
71 Slow equines

DOWN

1 Unappetizing food
2 Gridders' grp.
3 Baloney
4 Unspoken
5 Office workers of the past
6 Actor Rob
7 Type style: Abbr.
8 Winning sequence
9 Ostentatious displays
10 "The Aba __ Honeymoon"
11 Peaceful
12 River to the Missouri
13 Guzzlers
21 Fraction of a ruble
22 Devastation
23 Nonsense, to a Brit
24 Word form for "ear"
29 Poet's contraction
30 Giraffelike animal
32 "__ Rhythm"
34 Rotisserie need
36 Soldier's lodging
38 Ryan or Tatum
39 Slot insert
40 Couch parts
41 Dye
42 Medical coverage grps.
46 Likelihood
47 Poster word
48 It's full of garbage
49 __ Mary (drink)
50 Track wager
54 Aboveboard
56 Inventor Howe
58 __ mater
59 Liver: Fr.
60 Landers and Miller
64 Not-so-hot grade
65 Hosp. areas

by Shirley Soloway

ACROSS

1 Pre-Easter season
5 "Oops!"
9 Elec. units
13 Potpourri
14 Beast
15 Rhythm
16 Apollo 11 astronaut
18 Basso Pinza
19 Fruity cooler
20 Boxer Sonny
21 Bible book
22 Promote new undergrowth
24 Biological partitions
26 Crossword fans
29 Penpoint
32 Arizona Indian
35 Shoe width
36 Yours, once
38 Neat as __
39 Handed out cards
42 *A Man __ Woman*
43 Measuring device
45 Clock numeral
46 Antique autos
47 Dispenser candy
48 Steal, in a way
52 Shock
54 African nation
58 Mama's mate
60 Pertaining to milk
63 Hosp. employees
64 Yale students
65 Star shortstop
67 Matures
68 Some tides
69 Ranch mom
70 Letter enclosure: Abbr.
71 Goofs up
72 Son of Seth

DOWN

1 Of a lung area
2 Steer clear of
3 Lawyer Louis
4 From A __
5 Commands: Abbr.
6 Injured
7 Futile
8 Actress Marilu
9 Red as __
10 Stadium level
11 Duet
12 Greek portico
14 Attacked
17 Manager Felipe
23 Express a view
25 CA zone
27 Zuider __
28 Take off
30 __-European (language family)
31 Arthur and Lillie
32 Door fastener
33 Mayberry child
34 Italian food
37 Sultan's pride
40 Columnist Smith
41 States of agitation
44 Tie silk
49 Molly of song
50 Sports jacket
51 Varnish ingredients
53 Out of style
55 Skater Boitano
56 Opening bars
57 Fireplace residue
58 Pod occupants
59 Seaweed
61 Emperor
62 Gratuities
66 Mrs., in Marseilles

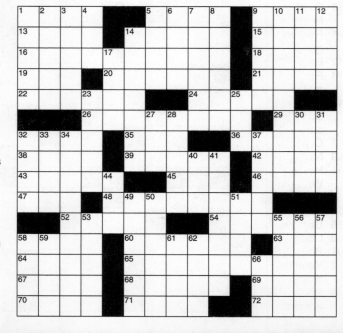

57 THE GAME'S AFOOT

by Lee Weaver

ACROSS

1 Wane
4 Headquarters
8 Dip out water
12 Intersection sign
15 Verve
16 Not fooled by
17 One at lunch
18 Donate
19 Face shape
20 Jockey Willie
22 Cash drawer
23 Lucid
24 "Gosh!"
26 Like sateen
30 Gomer of TV
31 Volcano output
32 Hodgepodge
35 Everglades bird
39 Portent
40 Fuss and feathers
41 Redcoat general
42 Bearlike beast
44 Roy Rogers' mate
46 Business-school subj.
47 Cohort
49 Nab
51 Half a Washington city
53 Certain
55 Demonstrate
56 Lifts weights
61 Poi source
62 Vacation option
63 Spiritual advisers
65 Chorus voice
66 Leer at
67 Has to have
68 Necklace component
69 Jury member
70 Match a raise

DOWN

1 Hurricane center
2 Prejudice
3 Sibling of Jo, Amy, and Meg
4 Started
5 Share and share __
6 Rescue
7 Pep
8 Rumrunner
9 Blacksmith's shaper
10 Neighbor of France
11 Laze (about)
13 Zodiacal lion
14 Frock or gown
21 Bread spread
25 Flamenco dancer's shout
26 Muck
27 Tibetan monk
28 Cookie cooker
29 Aromatic evergreen
30 Swimming site
33 Godiva, for one
34 Actress Lupino
36 Slalom or regatta
37 Selves
38 Camper's quarters
43 Nothing's alternative
45 "Lend me your __"
48 Portable PC
50 Rule
51 Moby Dick, e.g.
52 Main artery
53 Show pleasure
54 Berth place
55 Wild guess
57 Craving
58 Feel remorse
59 Mine finds
60 Hosiery shade
64 U-turn from NNW

by Chuck Deodene

ACROSS
1 Tête-à-tête
5 Painter Chagall
9 Big name in TV talk
14 Fattening
15 On a cruise
16 Mania
17 Tapered sword
18 David Geddes song of 1975
20 Enthusiasm
22 Jethro __ of rock
23 Letters before esses
24 Depth-finding instrument
25 Haphazard
27 Desert beast
29 __ 17 (Holden film)
33 Eschewers of pleasure
36 Frost
37 Illinois city
38 Royal headband
40 French friends
41 "Call it in the air" event
43 Tranquillity
46 Gut feeling
47 Peabrain
49 Blood vessel
53 __ Lingus
56 Fraud
57 Strengthen by tempering
58 1959 Godard film
61 Hammerhead's kin
62 Bring together
63 Faucet problem
64 Gulf of __ (Arabian Sea arm)
65 Copier chemical
66 Dory propellers
67 Pacific goose

DOWN
1 Salad green
2 Zoo heavyweight
3 __ the hole (secret weapon)
4 Jack Jones song of '65
5 Trade center
6 Tempe school: Abbr.
7 Hertz offerings
8 Louisiana cooking style
9 Spotted cat
10 Be too inquisitive
11 __ avis
12 Sky color, in Paris
13 They're fowl
19 Delta 88 maker
21 Angry
25 VCR button
26 '76 Hoffman thriller
28 Cambridge sch.
30 Italian resort
31 Singer Ed
32 Precious stones
33 Not quite shut
34 A number of
35 Remove, as a coupon
38 Uproar
39 Like Cuzco ruins
41 Fantastic dream
42 Unconscious
44 Lisa, to Bart Simpson
45 Carve in stone
48 Ralph __ Emerson
50 *The Cloister and the Hearth* author
51 Occupied, as a seat
52 Solo
53 Share a border
54 Cube maker Rubik
55 Harness part
57 Nile reptiles
59 Consumed
60 Dubbed title

59 BED TIME

by Bob Lubbers

ACROSS

1 Frolic
5 Volcano flow
9 Prefix for "within"
14 Moa cousin
15 "Oh, sure!"
16 Water duct
17 Top rating
18 Quarterback Starr
19 Dominican Republic neighbor
20 Tennis boo-boo
23 D.C. lobby
24 Bouncy melody
25 Singer Sheena
27 Fix a shoe
30 Page size
32 Actor Wallach
33 Approximately
35 Filled with fear
38 Script entries
40 God: Lat.
41 Mediterranean island
42 Safecracker
43 Afternoon nap
45 Bled, as dye
46 Triangular sail
48 Loosens forcibly
50 "That's water over __"
52 Uncountable years
53 NFL official
54 Subantarctic bird
60 In reserve
62 Med. school class

63 *The Thin Man* dog
64 Edmonton athlete
65 Medieval weapon
66 They follow effs
67 Fruit skins
68 Pitcher
69 Humorist Bombeck

DOWN

1 Peruse
2 Melville novel
3 Entrée list
4 Colorado city
5 Defamer
6 Toward the stern
7 Actress Miles
8 Aleutian island
9 Hoffman/Beatty film
10 Teachers' org.
11 World Trade Center, familiarly
12 Braking rocket
13 Suffix for sect
21 Actresses Kedrova and Lee
22 Conduct
26 Headliner
27 Count (on)
28 Writer Wiesel
29 Narrow march formation
30 Elizabeth, e.g.
31 Spanish ones

34 Garfield's pal
36 State: Fr.
37 Lairs
39 Old oath
41 Leslie of *Gigi*
43 Big rig
44 Audio-speaker feature
47 They'll bet
49 Hire
50 Scout group
51 Skater Sonja
52 Quickly
55 Title
56 Chew on, with "at"
57 Employer
58 Gossip tidbit
59 *Discovery* grp.
61 Cartoon unit

60 FRIGHTFUL

by Diane C. Baldwin

ACROSS

1 Snaillike
5 Computer message
10 Burn slightly
14 __ colada
15 Heavenly food
16 The __ Ranger
17 Waker-upper
19 Assns.
20 Ode to joy
21 Menu item
23 In the know
26 For each
27 Lock opening
28 Is of use
30 Life's work
31 Twist or frug
32 Usual routine
33 Conciliatory bribe
36 Adams or Brickell
37 Scamp
38 Bangkok native
39 Part of a min.
40 Ward off
41 Bullwinkle, e.g.
42 Theodore Cleaver
44 Cat, often
45 Dove (in)
47 Auction action
48 Draft org.
49 Roadside eyesore
50 Unbroken
52 Against
53 Cornfield protectors
58 Composer Stravinsky
59 Boring tool
60 Opera highlight
61 Not any
62 Clues of news
63 Fellow

DOWN

1 Fitness center
2 __ Abner
3 "__ Clear Day . . ."
4 Buckle
5 Roast hosts
6 Of the cheek
7 Shortly
8 Corp. name ender
9 Sight from Buffalo
10 Accouter
11 Scary films
12 Play backer
13 Attend again
18 "__ Leaf Rag"
22 Yeltsin turndown
23 Mythical underworld
24 Get away from
25 Alarm activator
27 Afghani capital
29 Drink cooler
30 Basketball player
32 Expected
34 Desert spots
35 Ships' landing places
37 Turnaround
38 Also
40 Violent anger
41 Army corpsman
43 Complete
44 Long-distance runners
45 Without frills
46 Special vocabulary
47 Not amused
50 Epic tale
51 Bummer
54 Pool tool
55 Unrefined metal
56 Come out on top
57 Waited

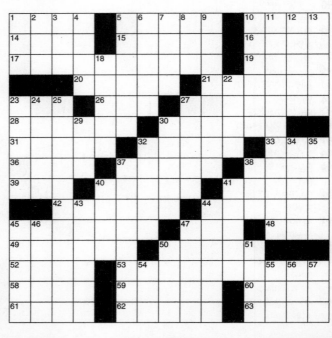

61 ANTE UP

by Bob Lubbers

ACROSS

1 The two
5 Small bite
8 Barter
13 Creme cookie
14 __ Alto, CA
15 Sponsorship
16 Beige
17 "Who __?" (knock response)
18 Limas and soys
19 Rant and rave
22 *"__, Brute?"*
23 Hockey great Bobby
24 Flightless bird
27 Texaco rival
30 __ worse than death
32 German surname starter
33 Navigation aid
34 Weather-map line
36 Seed covering
37 Wager
38 Theater grp.
39 Landed, as a trout
42 Slammin' Sammy
43 Traveler's stop
44 Actress Radner
46 Confound
47 Army bunk
48 Hair goo
49 Jacob's wife
51 Cruise game
56 Make happy
59 Hurler Hershiser
60 Waikiki party
61 Radio and TV
62 Camera eye
63 Faucet fault
64 Cutlass or épée
65 __ Moines, IA
66 Rational

DOWN

1 Afrikaner
2 Killer whale
3 Garr or Hatcher
4 Doctor's visit
5 New Hampshire city
6 Nastase of tennis
7 Braised beef
8 Type of stool
9 Atoll barrier
10 Turkish official
11 Racket
12 Double curve
14 Brad of *Seven*
20 British prep school
21 "__ take arms against a sea of troubles": Shak.
24 Tied (up)
25 Human
26 Sloppy, like a bed
27 Visigoth king
28 Actress Rita
29 East Asia
31 Devil
35 Climber's grips
37 Wallet
40 Intellectual
41 God: Fr.
42 Swedish car
45 Funt and Drury
50 Morays
51 Agitate
52 Set loose
53 Ambiance
54 April forecast
55 Fool
56 El followers
57 Ayres or Wallace
58 Fuss

62 LET'S FACE IT

by Lee Weaver

ACROSS

1 Stinging insect
5 Shoulder covering
10 __ up (finished)
14 Canyon effect
15 *M*A*S*H* setting
16 *Jane* __ (Brontë book)
17 Intimidated by a bully
19 Uncluttered
20 Comprehend
21 Out of kilter
22 Loses vitality
24 Winter vehicle
25 Sip loudly
26 Hesitate
29 Edinburgh native
30 Mrs. Perón
33 Other name
34 Lasting impressions
35 Silent assent
36 Imitate
37 Beagle or basset
38 Hung on to
39 Naval rank: Abbr.
40 Passed out the cards
41 Blacksmith's furnace
42 Shirt shape
43 Rank above viscount
44 Salad type
45 Enjoys a book
47 Dull sound
48 Reno's locale
50 Bearing
51 Kimono sash
54 Go off-stage
55 Indulged in idle gossip
58 Kitchen spice
59 Door part
60 Alternatively
61 Augury
62 Trimmed the lawn
63 Arizona city

DOWN

1 Spider's creations
2 *God's Little* __
3 Foot covering
4 "Wham!" relative
5 Shish kebab need
6 Accumulation
7 Pretentious
8 Like Willie Winkie
9 Rent collector
10 Spanish gent
11 Surprising bits of news
12 Decorate a gift
13 Knicks' rivals
18 Hay units
23 Wagon-wheel paths
24 Remain
25 Meager
26 Aspect
27 Unaccompanied
28 Insincere expression of loyalty
29 Light racing boat
31 Russian river
32 Viper
34 Flies like an eagle
37 Aspirin target
38 Worked in the garden
40 __ duck (goner)
41 Regional animals
44 Masticated
46 Gone from the plate
47 Hint of tint
48 *Nautilus* captain
49 Test
50 Chinese dynasty
51 Leer at
52 Mrs. Truman
53 Concept
56 Stashed away
57 Opal, e.g.

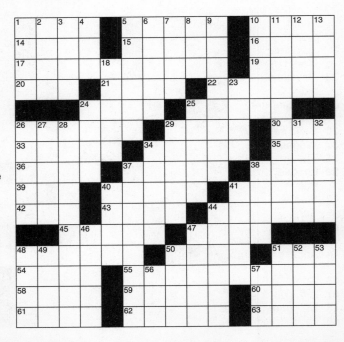

63 SUITE TALK

by Bob Lubbers

ACROSS

1 Patriot Nathan
5 FDR veep John __ Garner
10 XXV × X
13 "I __ return"
15 Yale or Root
16 __ polloi
17 Restaurant mingler
19 High card
20 Self-esteem
21 Mythical hunter
23 Predicaments
27 La Scala offerings
28 MGM mascot
29 Examination
30 Reindeer herder
31 Flightless bird
32 Belgian port
34 Singer McEntire
37 More kind
39 Prefix for center
40 Sophia of *Two Women*
41 Grey
42 Fix a sandal
44 Pose
45 Bosc or Bartlett
47 "Oh, sure!"
48 Single
49 Scoffs at
51 Mesh material
53 Untrue
54 Rev, as a motor
55 "__ Yankee Doodle Dandy"
56 Grounded pilots
64 Caress
65 "Doe, __ . . ."
66 Weird
67 Sold-out sign: Abbr.
68 Grassy spreads
69 Bumper bump

DOWN

1 FDR successor
2 "So *that's* it!"
3 Science room, for short
4 *Oklahoma!* aunt
5 Word form for "recent"
6 Swiss peak
7 __ in the bud
8 Fidel's pal
9 A moon of Jupiter
10 Committee head
11 Hot chocolate
12 Property claims
14 One who bequeaths
18 Aspirations
22 Printer's copy
23 Big rigs
24 TV junkie
25 Cosmetician Lauder
26 Substitutes (for)
27 Passé
28 Singer Horne
33 Weeper of myth
35 Existence
36 Penny-__ (minor)
38 Starers
40 Salad bed
42 Short Line and B&O
43 Release
46 Of an electrode
49 Quick cuts
50 Up-and-__ (rising star)
52 Signed, slangily
57 Writer LeShan
58 Use a needle and thread
59 Barbie's beau
60 Next year's seniors: Abbr.
61 Before, poetically
62 Yang's partner
63 Tennis unit

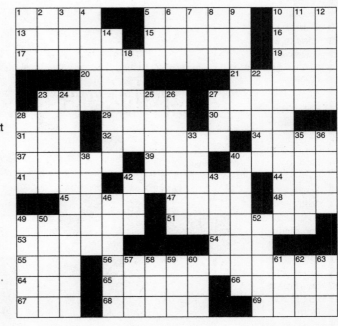

64 IN THE MIDDLE

by Elizabeth C. Gorski

ACROSS

1 H.S. exam
5 Workmen's __
9 Vowel sound
14 Police calls: Abbr.
15 Confirm
16 Contend
17 Floppy __
18 Billy goat or tomcat
19 Poker ploy
20 E.T.'s transport
21 Hearty ho-hos
23 Social event
25 Enervates
26 Darted
29 Seesaw
33 Destined
35 __ Mongolia
37 News org.
38 Haley or Trebek
39 Carrier
40 "Yes to that!"
41 Distress
42 Kirsten of *Little Women*
43 Clocked
44 President Mandela
46 Birthday frequency
48 Monogram part: Abbr.
50 Tootsie portrayer
53 Overeater's complaint
58 One for Carmen
59 Small: Fr.
60 Land mass
61 251 in old Rome

62 Writer Zola
63 At hand
64 Instruments for Tiny Tim
65 Checked out the joint
66 Willing
67 Spanish direction

DOWN

1 Italian city
2 Spruce (up)
3 Top-selling workout video
4 "Shame on you!"
5 Tourist's takealong
6 Like Truman's office
7 Pell-__ (disorderly)
8 Hunts, with "on"
9 Driver's winter need
10 Contract unit
11 Former Secretary of State
12 Hope
13 Singer Ed
21 Macaw or thrush
22 Not now
24 Top
27 Common lunch hour
28 Brave
30 Diet alternatives
31 Dueler's foil
32 Fruit skin
33 Young deer
34 Medicinal plant
36 Head: Fr.
39 Loose-fitting garment
40 Is unwell
42 Gave (to)
43 Loyal
45 "Sharp as a tack," e.g.
47 Cling (to)
49 Object
51 Small bay
52 Loud sounds
53 Architect's guideline
54 Musical motif
55 Elevator man
56 On the briny
57 Chowder base
61 Pool stick

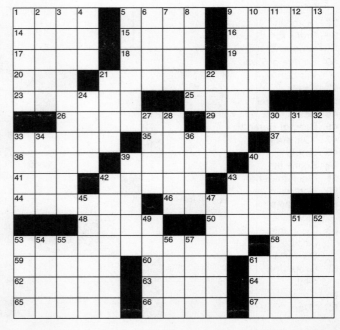

65 SMILE!

by Shirley Soloway

ACROSS

1 Sport hats
5 Pays attention to
10 Collections
14 Just __ (slightly)
15 Embellish
16 Light tan
17 Mr. __ (Lorre character)
18 Diva Callas
19 Winged
20 *Bye Bye Birdie* song
23 Mexican money
24 Diner patron
25 Backslide
28 "Fuzzy Wuzzy was __"
31 Muslim bigwig
32 Talked monotonously
35 Corn portions
39 Puts up with something
42 Price reduction
43 Get a new tenant
44 Tax preparer: Abbr.
45 Migrating birds
47 Earthy yellow
49 Skirt feature
52 Ashen
54 Is vindicated
61 Ratio phrase
62 Singing sounds
63 "Vamoose!"
64 Sly look
65 Edge (around)
66 Continental prefix
67 Raw metals
68 What the nose knows
69 Molt

DOWN

1 Summer destination
2 __ ben Adhem
3 Actor Brad
4 Bends down
5 Papas' costars
6 Potato variety
7 Nick Charles' wife
8 Faucet defect
9 Break apart
10 Mariner
11 Brilliance
12 Least remnant
13 More certain
21 Must have
22 Affirmative vote
25 Falls behind
26 Taj Mahal city
27 Bucket
28 Court star Agassi
29 Actress Daniels
30 Genesis locale
33 Uncommon
34 Wallet items
36 Writer Sholom
37 Prime for picking
38 Lead player
40 Voiders
41 Coral reef
46 Addis Ababa's country: Abbr.
48 Puts an end to
49 Detective Vance
50 Intense light
51 First name in cosmetics
52 Religious song
53 Confused
55 *Born Free* lioness
56 Home for 55 Down
57 Actor Ray
58 "I don't think so!"
59 Senate VIP
60 Parka part

by Fred Piscop

ACROSS

1 Coolidge, for short
4 Finish
9 Pay increase
14 River: Sp.
15 String quartet member
16 Stevens of *The Farmer's Daughter*
17 Farm equine
18 Stocking stuffer, perhaps
20 Parasite
22 Color range
23 Suit material
24 Computer unit
25 Loon relative
28 Fire sign
32 Whip
35 String tie
37 Singer O'Day
39 Inert
42 Beach Boy Wilson
43 Hard work
44 Gossipy Barrett
45 Foy or Arcaro
47 "Cool!"
49 Ship's pole
51 Church area
55 Curtail
59 Not the real thing
61 Beyond difficulty
63 Arguer's word
64 Repudiate
65 Aladdin's servant
66 Before
67 In bundles
68 Silvery fish
69 Extremist, informally

DOWN

1 Shellfish
2 Walkway
3 Also-ran
4 One that got away
5 Lake Nasser locale
6 Moody
7 City on the Danube
8 Abner's dad
9 Chuck Connors TV show, with *The*
10 Noun-forming suffix
11 "__ Rhythm"
12 Rush-hour prize
13 Perry's penner
19 Horse fodder
21 Intellectual
24 Triple Crown track
26 Fade away
27 Boxing event
29 Performing well
30 About 2.2 pounds
31 School founded by Henry VI
32 Legal deg.
33 Leeds' river
34 Slip, as on ice
36 Mayberry name
38 __ Khan
40 Lively
41 Slangy suffix
46 Apiece
48 Machine part
50 Keel extensions
52 Rome's river
53 Legend maker
54 Gave a PG to
55 Tiger Hall-of-Famer
56 Eye part
57 Swiss archer
58 Salted cheese
59 Secret writing
60 Pianist Gilels
62 Sewing job

67 DIZZY

by Bob Lubbers

ACROSS

1 Saudi, for one
5 Swedish rock group
9 Syrian president
14 Memo
15 Achiever
16 Overly sentimental
17 Pre-CD need
19 Layers
20 Old tar
21 Korean, e.g.
23 Talk like Daffy Duck
26 Barter
28 Irving Berlin song
32 Distant
34 Food plans
35 Homer epic
37 Half a dance
38 __ mater
39 Obdurate
40 Sky twinkler
41 Arafat's org.
42 Moisten, as meat
43 Swiss river
44 Metal worker of a sort
46 Materialized
48 Piano piece
49 Attempt
50 Goods
52 Unseat
57 Organic acid
59 Flighty person
62 Maine bay
63 Top-notch

64 Choir voice
65 Carved pole
66 Howard and Maynard
67 Comprehends

DOWN

1 Picnic pests
2 Dissolute one
3 Shaver brand
4 Road curve
5 Slow tempo
6 Dole or Denver
7 Barbara __ Geddes
8 Vicinity
9 Had hopes
10 Dar es __

11 Press agent, perhaps
12 Imitate
13 Word form for "bad"
18 Bridge fares
22 Wander off
24 Angry moods
25 Jai alai balls
27 Fuel gas
28 Conform
29 Comic Bea
30 Cocktail garnish
31 __ glance (instantly)
33 Like some seals

36 All thumbs
39 Delhi dress
40 __ Na Na
42 Apartment part
43 Revolt
45 Nicety
47 Chaplains
51 Envelope acronym
53 Lindstrom and Zadora
54 Stare at
55 Location
56 Self-images
57 Play segment
58 __ Zedong
60 Garden tool
61 Wayside stopover

ACROSS

1 Endure
5 Common mineral
9 Banal
14 Wheel holder
15 Russian river
16 Sweltering
17 Children's game
19 Silly
20 Greek H
21 Calendar abbr.
22 Crew member
24 Bagel centers
26 Somewhat: Suff.
27 Counsel
30 New Jersey city
35 Semiconductor, e.g.
36 English composer
37 Emerald Isle
38 Put on board
39 Tiny insects
40 Formulate
41 "__ Dinka Doo" (Durante song)
42 Cuts down
43 French seaport
44 Boston nickname
46 Seeks pests, as a cat
47 __ Plaines, IL
48 Crave
50 Storage spaces
54 Diagnostic aid: Abbr.
55 Not at home
58 Waterproof fabric
59 Sidewalk game

62 South American range
63 Word form for "straight"
64 Farm structure
65 Annoying
66 "__ Little Tenderness"
67 Genesis man

DOWN

1 Army camp
2 Theater sign
3 __ mater
4 Pierce Arrow rival
5 Triceps, e.g.
6 Wrathful
7 Island
8 As well
9 Want for water
10 Backyard game
11 Muslim prayer leader
12 Turner or Louise
13 *Paradise Lost* locale
18 Rope loop
23 Buenos __
24 Kindergarten game
25 Gaunt
27 Wing it
28 Sawyer of ABC News
29 Clear liquor
31 Hill dwellers
32 Miffs
33 Remove
34 Canvas homes
36 Once more

39 "Great Caesar's __!"
43 __ acid (antiseptic)
45 Quite small
46 Actress Mason
49 Needing refueling
50 Express approval
51 Solitary
52 Likelihood
53 Photograph
55 Cornelia __ Skinner
56 Bruins' sch.
57 You, once
60 Hockey great
61 Sugar suffix

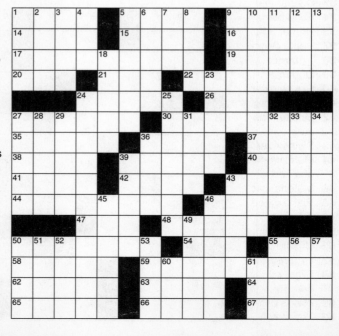

69 GROUND ROUND

by Bob Lubbers

ACROSS

1 Mardi __
5 Diplomat Eban
9 Bothersome
14 Actor Calhoun
15 Black: Fr.
16 Ne plus __ (the best)
17 Mosque official
18 Jest
19 Ashcan School painter John
20 Golfer's mecca
23 Ending for beat or peace
24 Unctuous
25 Eightsomes
27 Atom centers
30 Soap ingredient
32 __ Well That Ends Well
33 Put on ice
35 Donna and Rex
38 "__ pig's eye!"
39 Ad-hoc baseball field
41 Prefix for wit or pick
42 Apply, as varnish
44 Actor Richard
45 Tommie of baseball
46 Make glad
48 Clown Kelly
50 Indulged one's ego
52 Suit to __
53 Floor covering
54 Small hen
60 Too big
62 Good-deed doer
63 Parcel (out)
64 Deck
65 Prayer ender
66 And others: Abbr.
67 Puts in the mail
68 Durante's famous feature
69 Moist

DOWN

1 Take rudely
2 Italy's capital
3 Mubarak, e.g.
4 Emblems
5 Actress Huston
6 __ prize (loser's award)
7 Kid's vehicle
8 Vicinity
9 Sidewalk fruit stand
10 Building addition
11 English landmark
12 Characteristic
13 Pulls at
21 Untruth
22 Army bunk
26 Mao __-tung
27 Hammer target
28 Arm bone
29 Flying target
30 Hodge partner
31 Cooking pot
34 Singles
36 Weight-loss program
37 Proofreader's word
39 Those with nasty looks
40 Kind of correspondence
43 Used
45 Changed
47 Fuss
49 Mal de __
50 College teachers, for short
51 Moscow money
52 Farm land
55 Sleuth Charlie
56 __ Sabe (Tonto's pal)
57 Bit
58 Bridge feat
59 Aid
61 Grass square

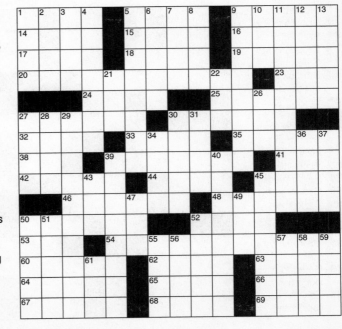

ROYAL SUBJECTS

by Rich Norris

ACROSS

1 Bounder
4 Show relief
8 Drive-in employee
14 Summer drink
15 Not in port
16 Think
17 "Stand By Me" singer
19 Grownups
20 Food
21 Notice
22 Meek as a __
23 Scram ending
25 Dock
27 Tennis officials
30 Sort
33 Antic
36 Word weaver
37 Dundee denial
38 Topped with ice cream
41 Mottled
43 Sprat's taboo
44 Partner of Crosby and Stills
46 Stadium sections
47 Ending for differ
48 Actually there
51 Swimming-lesson place
53 Account exec
54 Parlor piece
58 Green gem
60 "__ a true story"
62 Visual
65 *Hawaii Five-O* star
66 Develop a liking for
67 To __ (perfectly)
68 Actress Charlotte
69 Unyielding
70 Ancient Persian
71 Part of CBS

DOWN

1 Conspiratorial group
2 __ Rogers St. Johns
3 Jeans fabric
4 Rice drink
5 Has knowledge of
6 Not harsh
7 Witch
8 U.S. spy grp.
9 Tack on
10 Get more out of
11 Tony-winning director
12 Preminger or Klemperer
13 Harasser
18 Badge, e.g.
24 African snake
25 Apple skin
26 Wholly
28 Funny, sort of
29 Unruly group
31 Cowardly Lion actor
32 C major and A minor
33 Small restaurant
34 Alda or Thicke
35 Oscar winner as Helen Keller
39 Carvey or Delany
40 Sixth sense
42 Holiday hanging
45 That woman
49 Buyer's enticement
50 Kept apart
52 Donnybrook
55 Aromas
56 Organized assault
57 Chilean mountain range
58 Scribbles (down)
59 Room to swing __
61 __-ball (arcade game)
63 Part of NATO
64 Clark or Orbison
65 Causeway congestion

71 READING MATTER

by Rich Norris

ACROSS

1 Fellow
5 Mama's mate
9 Bonnie's partner
14 Lofty
15 San __ Obispo, CA
16 Parka parts
17 Sandwich cookie
18 Picnic pests
19 Mythical monsters
20 Followed established procedure
23 Mall units
24 *Treasure Island* monogram
25 __ Paulo, Brazil
28 Snake in the grass
29 Collar insert
30 *The Time Machine* monogram
31 Fiery felony
34 Underweight
35 Part of some phones
36 Detailed information
39 Roman historian
40 Diller's spouse
41 Bumbling
42 Chemical suffix
43 City north of Pittsburgh
44 Calendar abbr.
45 *The __ Squad* (TV oldie)
46 *A Few Good __*
47 Bob Marley's music
50 All along
54 Characteristic
56 Part in a play
57 Vicinity
58 Italian bowling
59 It rings the pupil
60 Exam
61 Looks for
62 Formal agreement
63 CPR givers, often

DOWN

1 Grub
2 Takes on
3 Ten-percenter
4 Duplicate, as a document
5 Game participant
6 Family members
7 Solidity
8 Speaking confidently
9 Persnickety
10 Corporate symbol
11 English county
12 HST follower
13 Double curve
21 Main force
22 Sans spice
26 Acting shocked
27 Nocturnal nestling
29 Ladd western
31 Happy as __
32 African beast
33 Avoided embarrassment
34 Excursion of a kind
35 Malign
37 Actor Zimbalist, Jr.
38 Last sign of summer
43 Overacts
44 Least
47 Dig find
48 Relevant, in legalese
49 Cast out
51 *Casablanca* role
52 Israeli dance
53 Stall sustenance
54 Cable network: Abbr.
55 Fish eggs

BAKER'S HALF-DOZEN

by Shirley Soloway

ACROSS

1 Roster
5 Significant
10 Ski lift
14 Ancient Peruvian
15 Cognizant
16 Actress Raines
17 Escape blame
19 Rain heavily
20 Moses crossed it
21 Citrus fruits
23 Promos
24 Mrs., in Madrid
26 Touch down
27 Affect adversely
30 Fraternal order member
33 Actor Rob
36 Dieters' retreats
37 Plymouth colonist
39 Anesthetic
41 NY zone
42 "Mule Train" singer
43 Short stalk
44 Flier's word form
46 TV interference
47 Call for help
48 Magazine features
51 Astute
53 *Jeanne*, e.g.
54 High __ kite
57 Tusked animal
59 First family of the 1870s
61 Whimper
62 Instigating
65 Jai __
66 Spooky
67 Hosiery shade
68 *The __ the Limit* (Astaire film)
69 Sipper's need
70 Org.

DOWN

1 Zodiac sign
2 "__ Your Love Tonight" (Presley tune)
3 A lot
4 Creates lace
5 George of *Route 66*
6 Fill with fear
7 Food container
8 Vocal
9 Throws off
10 Wyoming range
11 Became part of the group
12 Pub orders
13 St. Louis athlete
18 Hart cohost
22 Taj __
25 Charisma
27 Sob
28 Used a light beam
29 Houston team
31 Letterman rival
32 Was aware of
33 Not as much
34 Director Preminger
35 Snatch quickly
38 Highland miss
40 Pass along, as a client
45 Got too big for
49 Burdens
50 Garr or Hatcher
52 New York island
54 Cattle breed
55 Certain buttons
56 Colorado resort city
57 Bubbly bandleader
58 Printer's mark
60 __ *Karenina*
61 Barker and Bell
63 Not perf.
64 Stream

73 GROUND CREW

by Lee Weaver

ACROSS

1 Attempt
5 Rugged rock
9 Lima or soy
13 Cougars
15 First-rate
16 Bargain time
17 Leaning
18 Justice __ Bader Ginsburg
19 Singer Guthrie
20 Innovative blues musician
23 Nearly a dozen
24 Realty unit
25 Feeling restless
27 Farewell, in France
30 Sweater material
32 Singer Campbell
33 Poor, as an excuse
35 Black tea
38 Sushi servings
39 Fear
41 Pickling herb
42 Praise highly
44 "Do __ others . . ."
45 Part of a list
46 Frightens
48 Oven gloves
50 Too big
51 Egg layer
52 African antelope
53 *The Hogan Family* star
60 Ventilates
62 Appear
63 Stir up
64 Came to
65 Portent
66 Creepy
67 Leg joint
68 Shows agreement silently
69 Heavy metal

DOWN

1 Canned meat
2 Ballet costume
3 Surrounded by
4 Hairless
5 Diamond weight
6 One-sided fight
7 Start the pot
8 Babe Ruth teammate
9 Troop group: Abbr.
10 Sultry night-club singer
11 Bowling lane
12 Broadway light
14 Panache
21 Was willing to
22 Halt
26 Bank offering
27 *Jeopardy!* host Trebek
28 *Designing Women* star
29 Shoe part
30 Prayer endings
31 Nifty
32 "That's incredible!"
34 Calla-lily family
36 Toreador accolades
37 Shade tree
40 Round-topped
43 Glaswegian girl
47 Motive
49 Accustom
50 Burger topping
51 Sunday songs
52 Stare
54 *Nautilus* captain
55 Monopoly card
56 Christmas carol
57 Treat meat
58 India's location
59 Require
61 Catch sight of

74 POSTURING

by Bob Lubbers

ACROSS

1 Fashionable
5 Terrier of film
9 Of yore
14 Dynamics starter
15 Afternoon socials
16 __ Selassie
17 Unprosperous period
19 DXI × V
20 Ate well
22 Garfield's foil
23 Account subtractions
26 Two-year-old
28 Garden spot
29 Corn unit
32 Deuce topper
33 Bedsheets
35 Euripides tragedy
37 Educ. center
40 __ Gabler
41 Actress Gardner
42 Provoke
44 Word form for "equal"
45 Different
47 Harden (to)
48 Moniker
50 Meadow
52 Colorado resort
53 Linksman Lee
56 Shows of contempt
58 Ascend
59 Breathing tube
62 States firmly
64 Kids' game
68 "__ porridge hot . . ."
69 Singular person
70 Ade base
71 Cast about
72 Meeting point
73 Osprey cousin

DOWN

1 Presidential nickname
2 __ Haw
3 Lyricist Gershwin
4 Pent up
5 Resting
6 Red and Yellow
7 Sharply flavored
8 Poise, e.g.
9 Electrical unit
10 Pie à __
11 Nothing, slangily
12 J.R.'s mom
13 Not even once
18 Still
21 Indulge, with "on"
23 Indian metropolis
24 Adams and Brickell
25 Talk to tiresomely
27 Window cover
30 Asian nanny
31 Delight (in)
34 Singer Judd
36 Challenge
38 Radium researcher
39 Cads
43 Not capable of sustaining life
46 Circus shelter
49 Opposed
51 On land
53 Golf obstacles
54 Metal connector
55 Bean or Welles
57 Vim
60 __ cost (free)
61 Like some dorms
63 Stitch
65 Atmosphere
66 K followers
67 Bruce or Peggy

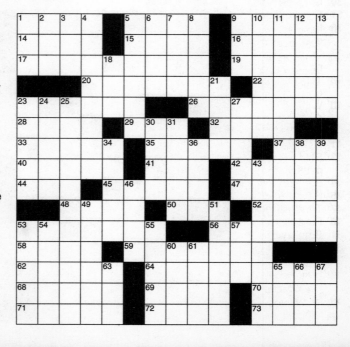

75 BEASTLY FOLKS

by Diane C. Baldwin

ACROSS

1 Skiing site
6 Show dismay
10 Tumble
14 Safe spot
15 Choir voice
16 Actress Perlman
17 Turn inside out
18 Clarinet adjunct
19 Long, long time
20 Unexpected victor
22 Sawyer or Keaton
23 Confident
24 Gave a nudge
26 High-school dance
29 Tennis unit
30 Not ambitious
31 Greet the day
33 Down in the dumps
37 "Three Bears" name
38 Tendon-bone connection
40 Woody Guthrie's son
41 Eases off
43 Stable partition
44 Bring up
45 High card
47 Thus far
48 Fast tempo
51 Sandwich fish
53 Church crosses
54 Roadside rogue
59 Singer Clapton
60 Alan of M*A*S*H
61 Tropical fruit
62 Roman despot
63 Food shop, for short
64 Modify
65 Once again
66 Utopia
67 *The Merry Widow* composer

DOWN

1 Cast off
2 Vesuvius output
3 All done
4 Makes java
5 Thrill
6 Artist's room, perhaps
7 Pale brews
8 Church tops
9 Pea holder
10 Timid chap
11 In the future
12 Sierra __
13 Like most highways
21 Lode stuff
22 Get forty winks
25 Indian prince
26 Deli meats
27 Kind of exam
28 Cotton variety
32 One immune from criticism
33 AMA members
34 Cafeteria carrier
35 *Vogue* rival
36 Clod
38 Smokey or Yogi
39 Opened a scroll
42 Beer holders
43 West African country
45 Reach
46 Director's cry
48 Bout site
49 Actress Sophia
50 France's longest river
52 As __ (generally)
55 Not active
56 Shower alternative
57 Eye feature
58 Teri of *Tootsie*
60 Lime drink

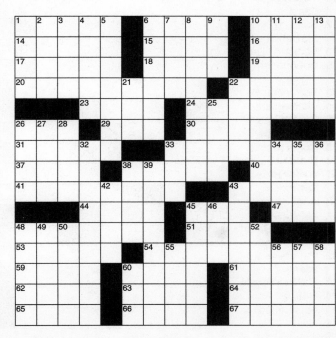

76 OOPS!

by Gerald R. Ferguson

ACROSS

1 Mil. branch
5 H.S. exam
9 Act stealthily
14 Saint Philip __
15 Doily material
16 Philadelphia gridder
17 General Bradley
18 "It's __ big mistake!"
19 Line of work
20 "Excuse me!"
23 Streetcar
24 Skater Midori
25 Dudley or Clayton
28 Nobleman
31 Spiders' snares
35 Peruvian beast
37 Saint, in Mozambique
38 Tankard filler
39 Spoonerism, e.g.
43 Soft metal
44 Wish undone
45 Sank a basket
46 Look (to be)
48 Some motels
50 Braid of hair
51 *NYPD Blue* network
53 Angelou or Frost
55 Maxwell Smart catchphrase
62 Put on, as a scene
63 Pollster Roper
64 Desire personified
66 Host

67 Nautical adverb
68 Clinton Attorney General
69 Fruit skins
70 June honorees
71 Henpecks

DOWN

1 One, in Rome
2 Prefix for sweet
3 Part of U.A.R.
4 Unsafe structure
5 Beach: Sp.
6 Strauss opera
7 Rights group: Abbr.
8 Rip
9 __ ease (make comfortable)
10 Like AAA shoes
11 "Yikes!"
12 Actor __ Ray
13 Sharp
21 El __ (painter)
22 Steers
25 Ships' poles
26 Hardy, to Stan
27 Express oneself
29 Visibly frightened
30 __ Dawn Chong
32 Tidal flood
33 Jazz form
34 Spring planting need
36 Togo's locale
40 Wine cask
41 Group of eight
42 What "borealis" means
47 Mime Marceau
49 Formed froth
52 Computer units
54 Oklahoma Indians
55 Flow slowly
56 "This one's __!" (treater's phrase)
57 Marathon, e.g.
58 Dewdrop
59 Stewpot
60 Sphere
61 Chinese secret society
65 Brillo alternative

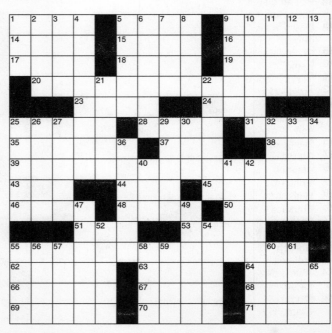

77 HEADS UP

by Bob Lubbers

ACROSS

1 Remove, as a hat
5 Singer Kay
10 Corn holders
14 Mine: Fr.
15 Indian dwelling
16 Opera solo
17 Lunch course
19 Repast
20 Actress Hawn et al.
21 Mattress support
23 Chop (off)
24 Mideast desert
25 ___-Powell (Scouts founder)
28 Darlin'
29 Savage
33 Western Indian
34 Bit of barbecue
35 Nabokov novel
36 Bonkers
40 Mixes
41 Psyche parts
42 Twist the truth
43 Eagle's nest
44 One of Mel's waitresses
45 Not cloudy
47 Expert group
49 Onassis, familiarly
50 Visits
53 Prickly shrub
57 Arizona Indian
58 Lanky one
60 Actress Barbara
61 Legal excuse
62 Director Preminger
63 Bell sound

64 Renter's paper
65 "___ only a bird in a . . ."

DOWN

1 "Doggone!"
2 Melville novel
3 Silly one
4 Monkey (with)
5 Exorbitant
6 Thomas Hardy heroine
7 Part of some GI addresses
8 Corned beef and cheese sandwich
9 Fix a floor, perhaps
10 Scottish surname
11 Cookie sandwich
12 Slant
13 Shaker contents
18 Disney's The ___ King
22 Crusoe's creator
24 San Francisco neighborhood
25 Good-ol'-boy nickname
26 ___ of Two Cities
27 Inhibit
28 ___ the books (study)
30 Army arm
31 Lofty hotel lobbies
32 Stratum
34 Med. professionals

35 Weight units: Abbr.
37 Cutting quickly
38 Brainstorms
39 Tokyo, once
44 Condition
45 Rocky cliff
46 Caribbean dances
48 Twangy
49 Golfer Palmer, to fans
50 Lean-to
51 Fuss
52 Unlock
53 Tots' coverings
54 Jo's sister
55 Tardy
56 Seth's son
59 Spanish creek

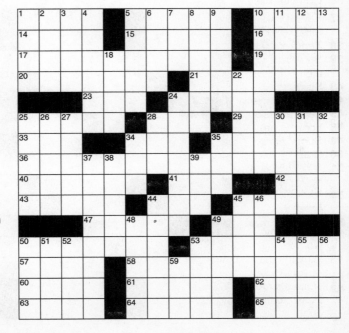

78 THRU THE RANKS

by Elizabeth C. Gorski

ACROSS

1 Afrikaner
5 Pines (for)
10 Uninteresting
14 Leer at
15 Limber
16 Do a yard chore
17 Goldie Hawn film
20 Bering, e.g.
21 55 Across under Reagan
22 Olympian Jesse
23 Catches some rays
24 Took a dive
26 Emphasis
29 Religious group
30 Computer key
33 Prepared baking apples
34 Ship's body
35 Choral voice
36 "Big show," to baseballers
39 Granola ingredient
40 Just
41 West Point student
42 U-turn from SSW
43 Dewey and Louie's brother
44 Apartment workers
45 Wealthy man of verse
46 Domesticated
47 Plowmaker John
50 Pickle juice
52 Oklahoma city
55 Cabinet member
58 Singer Phoebe
59 Lagers
60 Eliot's *Adam __*
61 Ranch helper
62 Resource
63 Bo Peep hears them

DOWN

1 Smacks in the noggin
2 Meanie
3 Director Kazan
4 Gun the engine
5 Unactualized
6 Double curves
7 Penpoints
8 With great joy
9 Rep.'s colleague
10 Free-for-all
11 Weak, as an excuse
12 Similar
13 Cluckers
18 Plummer of *The Fisher King*
19 Sudden impact
23 Comes down in buckets
25 Model Macpherson
26 Make happen
27 "Over There" composer
28 Largest Greek isle
29 Like permed hair
30 Give the slip to
31 Direct
32 Prices
34 Apiary residents
35 Wide open
37 Day: Fr.
38 Shrewdness
43 Soil worker
44 Most lucid
45 Mass of people
46 French beast
47 Morse unit
48 Sicilian volcano
49 British school
51 Sandwich breads
52 Vicinity
53 Baby's word
54 Pub pints
56 Hoopster's org.
57 Recede

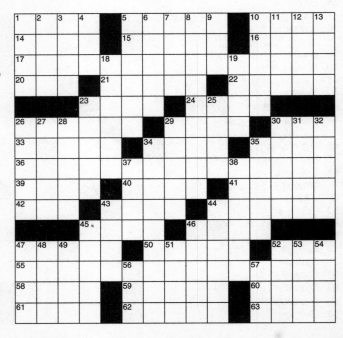

79 SLUGFEST

by Shirley Soloway

ACROSS

1 Sportscaster Albert
5 South African
9 "Splish Splash" singer
14 Opera solo
15 Singer Fitzgerald
16 Remove
17 Hold back
20 Beer mug
21 Aleutian island
22 Solidify
23 Part of a plan
26 Promos
28 Fail completely
36 Give __ whirl
37 Lord's house
38 Top quality
39 Ranee's wrap
41 Half a Latin dance
42 Bestow
43 Seafood fare
44 __-toity
46 Actress Scala
47 Attack unfairly
51 __-mo replay
52 Just fair
53 D'Amato and Gore
56 Actor Arkin
59 Give a speech
63 Do one's best
67 Getz and Musial
68 Icelandic literary work
69 Fräulein's refusal
70 Ghostlike
71 Consider

72 Rowlands of film

DOWN

1 Driver's aids
2 In __ (stuck)
3 Antagonize
4 Suitcase
5 Kingsley or Jonson
6 Grand __ Opry
7 Movie lioness
8 Engrossed
9 Lay bare
10 Circle segment
11 Stadium shouts
12 Words of comprehension
13 Heron's home

18 Prompt
19 Mormon state
24 Greek vowel
25 Sleeveless wrap
27 Look over
28 Larry of CBS
29 Computer name
30 Gold measure
31 "Impossible!"
32 Characteristics
33 Podge preceder
34 How some tuna is packed
35 Inexperienced with
40 Recedes

42 *The __ Laura Mars* (Dunaway film)
45 But, for short
48 Run out
49 Singer Falana
50 Uninteresting
53 Church area
54 Renaissance instrument
55 Night-sky sight
57 Matured
58 Plant protrusion
60 Film critic James
61 Willowy
62 Italian volcano
64 Cycle starter
65 Verse form
66 Hoover, for one

80 BATHDAY PRESENTS

by Lee Weaver

ACROSS

1 Man of morals
6 Revolutionary War general
10 Fisherman's maneuver
14 Reduced to fragments
15 Territory
16 Hoarfrost
17 Delete
18 Milky Way part
19 Sign of the future
20 Kitchen meas.
21 Handy wiper-uppers
24 Begins the bidding
26 Cope with
27 Call the strikes
29 Karpov's game
31 Film holder
32 Hula performer
34 Troop group: Abbr.
37 Young ladies
39 Food fish
40 Light racing boat
42 Notable period
43 Hall of Famer Spahn
46 Reed instrument
47 Like some coats
48 Baked bricks
50 Inquiring
53 Hardly huge
54 Light desserts
57 Freudian concept
60 Fabled race loser
61 Places
62 Navajo dwelling

64 East of __
65 Finished the cake
66 Spew forth
67 Red and Baltic
68 Scoundrels
69 Alfa __ (car)

DOWN

1 Help with the heist
2 Makes mistakes
3 Daily TV fare
4 Approvals, for short
5 Baby chick, e.g.
6 Sounds of surprise
7 Johnson of *Laugh-In*
8 Machine part

9 Made of baked clay
10 Tiaras, e.g.
11 Pointed (at)
12 Aroma
13 All wound up
22 All over again
23 Caravan stops
25 Medicinal medium
27 Coax
28 Golda of Israel
29 Tonal combination
30 Stay out of sight
33 Realty unit
34 Kid's jaw exerciser
35 Gin flavoring
36 Pub potables
38 Playground item

41 Swell, in the '50s and '90s
44 Heavenly
45 Moniker
47 Sheets and pillowcases
49 Dancer's partner
50 Campfire residue
51 Fictional detective Sam
52 Asian nation
53 Slips on the ice
55 Comedienne Imogene
56 Passed easily
58 Stare with dropped jaw
59 Aware of
63 Conquistador's quest

81 ON THE MOVE

by Diane C. Baldwin

ACROSS

1 Work hard
6 Work stint
11 Director Reiner
14 Higher than
15 Asian city
16 Bullring cry
17 Night traveler
19 Fruity quaff
20 Munich mister
21 Chichi
22 Birch kin
24 Faucet problem
26 Dresses up
27 Fish group
30 Part of FBI
32 Indicate, with "at"
33 Beer barrels
34 "Uh-uh!"
37 Advantage
38 Kathy of *Misery*
39 "Do __ others . . ."
40 Morse Code sound
41 Some coastal cities
42 Villain's look
43 Old car
45 California team
46 Main points
48 Chess-game conclusion
49 Hebrew letter
50 Flue dirt
52 Wily subterfuge
56 Little rascal
57 Green cocktail
60 Be in contention
61 National bird
62 TNT center
63 Poet's adverb
64 Chases off
65 Elitists

DOWN

1 Mascara target
2 Competent
3 South African settler
4 Cooked too much
5 House mem.
6 Pointy
7 Sentry's cry
8 Very dark
9 Antagonist
10 Verbal eruptions
11 Cartoon bird
12 Of bygone times
13 Malty drinks
18 Mournful noise
23 Mauna __
25 Disintegrate
26 Large vessels
27 Went lickety-split
28 Musical ending
29 Track athlete
30 Eccentric
31 Takes advantage of
33 Find fault
35 Suit to __
36 __ d'oeuvres
38 Cries of derision
39 Support, as a foundation
41 Promises
42 Took a chair
44 Logger's tool
45 Walkway
46 Novelist Cussler
47 Fabric fiber
48 Painter Grandma __
50 Kind of palm
51 European capital
53 No higher than
54 Eastern European
55 Love god
58 Cheering sound
59 Light-switch positions

82 VIRTUOUS

by Fred Piscop

ACROSS

1 Nettle
5 Perfecto, e.g.
10 Tough spot
13 You love: Lat.
14 Comfort
15 Environmental prefix
16 Mary Baker Eddy, for one
18 Greek P
19 Diatribe
20 Elephant, e.g.
22 Porters' relatives
23 German city
24 Sock mender
27 Monarch's spouse
30 Do a front-end job
31 Chunk of ice
32 Witch
34 Hold unrealistic expectations
38 Moo __ pork
39 Matterhorn's range
40 Sculptor Auguste
41 Dismays
44 Unruffled
45 Andy's pal
46 Sheriff's badge
47 Eye neighbors
50 Copper coating
53 Bunyan tool
54 Fund-raiser
58 Ms. Caldwell
59 Goddess of witchcraft
60 Rickey flavoring
61 Conclusion
62 Cosmetician Lauder
63 Jack of westerns

DOWN

1 Battle of Britain fliers: Abbr.
2 "Look at me, __ helpless . . ."
3 Secular
4 Alienate
5 '50s dorm denizens
6 Stevedores' grp.
7 "My __ Sal"
8 Colorless solvents
9 Summer TV fare
10 Dweeb
11 Post-workout woe
12 Anchor
14 Like some fabrics
17 Rubinstein of cosmetics
21 __-cone (ice treat)
23 Blessings
24 Morse bits
25 Hawaii "hi"
26 Tear apart
27 Evens the hedges
28 __ Island Red
29 Two-pointer
31 Niagara, e.g.
33 Wilder or Hackman
35 Rainy-day footwear
36 Versailles document
37 Abominable
42 Oom-__
43 Don of *Cocoon*
44 Aver
46 Ill will
47 Lounge around
48 Nerve-cell part
49 Feeder filler
51 Makeshift coat hanger
52 __ mater
55 Play a part
56 Comic Charlotte
57 Apollo component

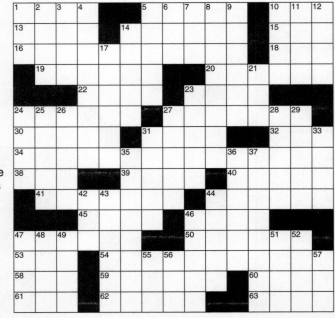

83 TABLE SETTING

by Rich Norris

ACROSS

1 Baby's word
5 Office item
9 Animal's stomach
13 Monogram part: Abbr.
14 Breathing sound
15 Urbane
16 Exemplar of dullness
18 Lively frolic
19 Lined up
20 Lined up
22 Knock down
24 Skirmish
25 Ticket leftover
27 Wisconsin college
29 Western alliance: Abbr.
30 AT&T rival
32 Most achy
35 Like better
37 "Neat!"
39 Aphrodite's love
41 Prefix for function
42 *Norma* __
43 Go back on one's word
45 Meadowlands team
46 Actor Gregory
49 Boxer's weak spot
52 Surgeon's tools
54 Piranha
57 Southwestern Indians
58 Pamper
60 Up in the air
61 Camp sight
62 Mil. coll.
63 Took off
64 Scraps for Fido
65 Former Ford models

DOWN

1 Conn of *Grease*
2 Has __ with (knows)
3 Freed from error
4 Pulsing
5 Slow speech
6 Dine
7 Jacket part
8 Corn bits
9 Personal preference
10 Less common
11 Oat grass
12 Overgrown, as a lawn
15 Fast flier: Abbr.
17 Amazed shout
21 Tired-looking
23 Japanese sash
25 Absorb, with "up"
26 Scarlett's home
28 Makes angry
30 Biblical graffiti word
31 Shrink away
33 Most outlandish
34 The other one
36 Warehouse device
38 "Sure!"
40 Does business with
41 __ Moines, IA
44 Horror film watcher, at times
45 Cookies quantity
46 Word of disapproval
47 French school
48 Kind of chicken
50 Glaswegians
51 First mo.
53 L.A. zone
55 Gentle curve
56 Author LeShan et al.
59 Ottawa's prov.

84 HAVE IT YOUR WAY

by Gerald R. Ferguson

ACROSS

1 Downturn
6 Church event
10 Schmo
14 Word before code or colony
15 Adjoin
16 Spiny houseplant
17 Palm Springs neighbor
18 Actress Miles
19 Kelly or Tunney
20 Boot tip
21 When to get it?
24 Uncle of fiction
26 Actress Gardner
27 Oklahoma Indian
29 Mighty
34 Wading bird
35 Back tooth
36 Cell chemical: Abbr.
37 Levin and Gershwin
38 __ Island (Big Apple resort)
39 Guzzlers
40 Sass
41 Madrid museum
42 Send payment
43 Meetings
45 Midler et al.
46 Med. insurance plan
47 Football coach Bill
48 How to do it?
53 Wriggly fish
56 On the briny
57 Once, old-style

58 Preface, for short
60 Waist cincher
61 Learning method
62 Sign gases
63 Clockmaker Thomas
64 Ship's mast
65 Is wide-eyed

DOWN

1 Shish-kebab need
2 Tonight Show host
3 Where to keep it?
4 __ tai (drink)
5 Tillers
6 Gospel singer Staples

7 Genesis name
8 Certain
9 Emulate a no-show
10 Panther kin
11 Util. product
12 Novelist Jaffe
13 Sharp
22 Color
23 Finished
25 Genesis figure
27 Silvers and Foster
28 Eagle's nest
29 Small lakes
30 Toast spread
31 Where to take it?
32 Open a bow
33 Endures

35 Groan's companion
38 Bing's emulators
39 Hardens
41 Egyptian cotton
42 Trusting, with "on"
44 Scabbard
45 Coll. degrees
47 Tend the plants
48 Arrests
49 Savvy reply
50 Ancient Briton
51 Bit of rain
52 This: Sp.
54 Sea eagle
55 Financial setback
59 PBS benefactor

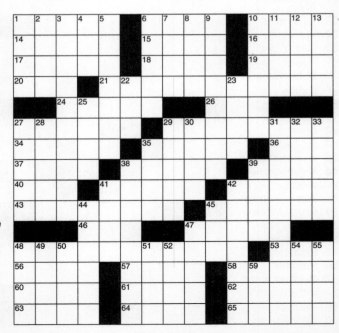

85 CONTAINMENT

by Shirley Soloway

ACROSS

1 Composers' org.
6 Greatest amount
10 Brad of *Seven*
14 Norse chieftain
15 Aroma
16 __ about (approximately)
17 WWII sub
18 Horne or Olin
19 Corn dish
20 Is dismissed
23 Actress Peeples
24 New Zealand parrot
25 Put back in office
27 Actor Jason
31 Understands
32 Wedding words
33 Decade parts
36 River to the Rio Grande
39 Schoolbook
41 Sugary
43 Govern
44 Eastern Indians
46 Wash vigorously
48 Pod veggie
49 Short snoozes
51 Window over a door
53 Skin coloring
56 "__ to Pieces" ('65 tune)
57 Goof up
58 Relevant example
64 Dog's wagger
66 Jamie of *M*A*S*H*
67 "The future __!"
68 __ time (never)
69 Sky bear
70 Green sauce
71 Table parts
72 Atl. crossers
73 Senator Kefauver

DOWN

1 Cut __ (dance)
2 "__ it!" ("Amen!")
3 Coagulate
4 *Northern Exposure* state
5 Ceramic ware
6 Underground dweller
7 Commemorative poems
8 Sub detector
9 Vestiges
10 Dad
11 Besotted
12 Pick-me-up
13 Nice surprise
21 Mythological underworld
22 Retain
26 Nasty look
27 Ceremony
28 Czech river
29 Tyson's milieu
30 Wood cutters
34 VCR button
35 Spanish muralist
37 Veggie spread
38 Garment line
40 Mule group
42 City on the Po
45 Architectural detail, for short
47 Scottish instrument
50 Mixups
52 Rope loops
53 Flower part
54 Hot under the collar
55 Peter and Ivan
59 Prefix for while
60 Lyricist Gershwin et al.
61 Part of MIT
62 Short letter
63 Pairs
65 __ Alamos, NM

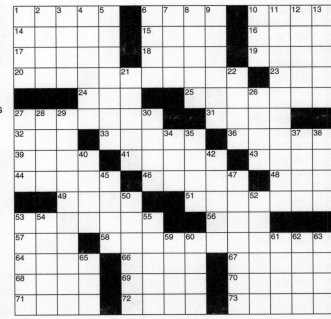

86 KENNEL RATION

by Randy Sowell

ACROSS

1 Singer Horne
5 Cowboy rope
10 Rotisserie part
14 "Take __ leave it"
15 Fiery felony
16 Hosiery shade
17 Ill-tempered one
19 Leer at
20 Japanese robe
21 Windflowers
23 Marmalade ingredient
25 Fizzy drink
26 Citadel student
29 Speedy biped
32 Tie type
35 Eros' Roman counterpart
36 Earth, e.g.
38 Certain savings plan: Abbr.
39 Russian jets
40 Ignited again
41 Bathday cake
42 Shade tree
43 Chip ingredient
44 Precious
45 Rent
47 Look at
48 Heston role
49 Eye drop
51 Expensive
53 Possums, for instance
57 Singer Lionel
61 For fear that
62 Dullard
64 Poker fee
65 Greek epic
66 Hence
67 Sit, as for an artist
68 __ Haute, IN
69 Ruin

DOWN

1 Wet an envelope
2 Small case
3 Standard
4 Knight suppliers
5 Dangerous gas
6 Work unit
7 On the ocean
8 Roger Rabbit, e.g.
9 Boleyn and Bancroft
10 Hairnets
11 Combative
12 Not at work
13 Golf props
18 Item
22 Castle protector
24 Strike out
26 Sahara beast
27 Missed by __
28 Doctrine-bound individuals
30 Asian peninsula
31 TWA rival
33 Speak pompously
34 Uses the VCR
36 In favor of
37 WWII command for DDE
41 Burned a bit
43 Garden need
46 Parlor piece
48 Principal
50 Send payment
52 Wear away
53 Applaud
54 Nevada city
55 Have dominion
56 Cooking direction
58 Large sandwich
59 Othello's undoer
60 Esau's country
63 Roof material

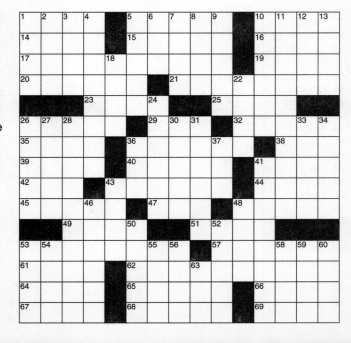

87 FARE IS FOWL

by Bob Lubbers

ACROSS

1 Within
5 Stitched line
9 Islamic center
14 Lucid
15 Sailors' saint
16 A Musketeer
17 Nagged
19 Have an opinion
20 Certain paints
22 Top cards
23 Legal adverb
26 Leg part
28 More than some
29 Talk-sing
32 Estimate
35 Blackthorn fruits
37 Requires
39 "It's __ for Me to Say"
40 Wimp
41 __ Aviv
42 Michael Caine role
44 Play part
45 Pours
47 Plow maker
48 __ with (encounter)
50 Droop
52 __-do-well
53 Uses a lasso
55 Awaits
57 Singer __ James
59 Gold-watch recipient
62 Lasso
64 Lamp type
68 Sign of the Ram
69 Cartoonist Peter
70 __ in (collapse)
71 Monica of tennis
72 Mortgage, for example
73 Ireland

DOWN

1 Bat wood
2 Ginnie __
3 Rural hotel
4 Uses up
5 Area
6 Actress Sommer
7 NYSE competitor
8 Fashions
9 Gym pad
10 Allen and Frome
11 Paltry amount
12 Ice-cream holder
13 Inquires
18 Consume
21 Roe source
23 Painter Childe __
24 __ Islands (former name of Tuvalu)
25 Speedboat's wake
27 Syrian president
30 Against
31 Hammer parts
33 Evening party
34 Takes the wheel
36 Waffle topper
38 *Born Free* lioness
43 Mercy
46 Copycat
49 Exactly
51 She played Mrs. Miniver
54 *Love Story* author
56 Honey maker
57 Time periods
58 Whitewall, e.g.
60 Matador's foe
61 New York campus
63 Wild equine
65 Jug handle
66 106, to Caesar
67 Author Kesey

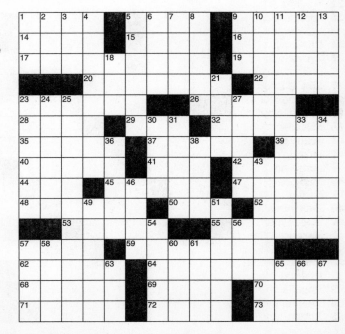

88 TOPOGRAPHICALS

by Gerald R. Ferguson

ACROSS

1 Religious service
5 Lead actor
9 Ugandan exile
13 *"Dies __"*
14 ". . . thereby hangs __"
15 Zilch
16 Singer Carter
17 *Salvador* star
19 Sailing ships
21 Ballroom dances
22 Egg parts
23 Optimistic
24 Say no
26 Xylophones' cousins
30 Top-drawer
31 Thesaurus compiler
32 __ Jima
33 Islands: Fr.
34 VCR input
35 Big family
36 Animator's unit
37 Like O'Brien potatoes
38 Fast dance
39 In a row
41 Participant
42 Like __ of sunshine
43 Muse of poetry
44 Grownups
47 Like some literary endings
50 *Pillow Talk* star
52 Pianist Peter
53 She: Fr.
54 Washer cycle
55 Strong wind
56 Scorch
57 Kitchen conclusion
58 Haughty one

DOWN

1 Flash Gordon's foe
2 Geometric calculation
3 *Norma Rae* star
4 Hit shows
5 Musial and Laurel
6 Scottish caps
7 Pub quaff
8 Puts back
9 Alias
10 Synthesizer creator
11 Subcontinental prefix
12 Famous T-man
14 "Can't you take __?"
18 "__ something I said?"
20 Alternatively
23 Threw a fit
24 Chill again
25 Actress Barkin
26 Acted pouty
27 "Suddenly" singer
28 Alert
29 Submarine finder
31 Prone to showers
34 Pirate's haul
35 Latex layers
37 Onward
38 Outline
40 Mynah or parrot
41 On one's stomach
43 Unevenly notched
44 War god
45 Campaign name
46 Bruins' sch.
47 "Ain't," correctly
48 Folk singer Guthrie
49 Leopold's partner
51 Telegraphy sound

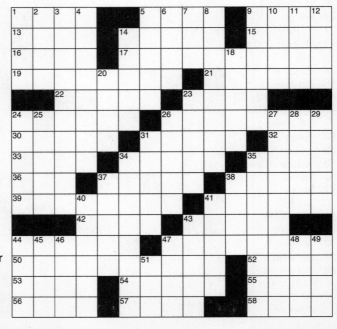

89 WATER PIX

by Lee Weaver

ACROSS
1 Amount paid
5 Merry pranks
10 Stinger
14 Fragrance
15 Goddess of peace
16 Hodgepodge
17 Himalayan legend
18 Even
19 Opera box
20 '60 Sinatra film
23 Where girls learn to swim
24 Army chow
25 Tango or twist
28 Mexican money
31 College exam
32 Drip source
34 Go out with
37 '54 Mitchum/ Monroe film
40 Merry month
41 Move swiftly
42 Peddle
43 Farm buildings
44 Woodworking tools
45 Acquire
47 18-wheeler
49 '81 Fonda/ Hepburn film
54 Former West German capital
55 Frightfully strange
56 Wine valley
59 India's location
60 Wed on the run

61 Spirit
62 Film holder
63 Stands up
64 Lease

DOWN
1 Flirtatious
2 Shelley poem
3 "And __ bed"
4 Tot's trans- portation
5 Pale purple
6 Stadium
7 Guns the engine
8 Leg joint
9 Deal in
10 *Dances With __*
11 African lilies
12 Portents

13 Mystery-story pioneer
21 Woolly one
22 Ham it up
25 Campus building
26 Diva's solo
27 Armada
28 Fourth-down plays
29 Environmental sci.
30 Dried out
32 Out of bounds, in baseball
33 Bushy hairdo
34 Egyptian canal
35 Sea eagle
36 Extremities
38 Horned animal

39 Frozen-food buy
43 Flare, e.g.
44 I love: Lat.
45 Golden-egg layer
46 Sharpshooter Oakley
47 Sandpiper
48 Fencing swords
50 Impolite look
51 Cold-cuts center
52 Aphrodite's child
53 Roy Rogers' wife
54 Saloon
57 Wok
58 Picnic pest

90 BURGER BUDDIES

by Patrick Jordan

ACROSS

1 Make fun of
5 Highest point
9 Around, to a historian
14 Like Clinton's office
15 Siren sound
16 Negatively charged atom
17 English essayist
20 Ames and Bradley
21 Tom Joad, for one
22 Midwest capital
23 "__ o'clock scholar"
24 Lotion additive
25 *Clue* character
31 Overactive, for short
32 Symbol of servitude
33 Soup veggie
34 Six-legged colonists
35 Reach home plate
37 Wild revelry
38 Reagan program: Abbr.
39 Course of action
40 Wanted-poster word
41 Buddy's wife on *The Dick Van Dyke Show*
45 Smell awful
46 Type of lily
47 Obliquely
50 Lhasa __
51 Greek letter
54 Clinic founders
57 Ore digger
58 Ship's timber
59 Wood cutters
60 Georgia university
61 Eye irritation
62 General's decoration

DOWN

1 San __, CA
2 Enthusiastic
3 Golfer's goals
4 Santa's helper
5 Heed the alarm
6 Pointed tooth
7 Lab rodents
8 Actor Wallach
9 Train ender
10 Sulking
11 Paddy crop
12 Chef
13 Paquin of *The Piano*
18 Helicopter part
19 N.T. author
23 Medieval quaffs
24 Latin love
25 Singer Lauper
26 Vision-related
27 Film critic Jeffrey
28 Spring month
29 Fit for a queen
30 Dennis and Doris
31 Door fastener
35 Like an icy downpour
36 Wine holder
37 Margarine
39 Fully attended
40 Jargon
42 Seinfeld's neighbor
43 Fish hawk
44 Mend a sandal
47 "Don't look __!"
48 Wood wedge
49 Late-night name
50 Help with a heist
51 Scriptural passage
52 Field of interest
53 Former UN member
55 Signs off on
56 Dines on

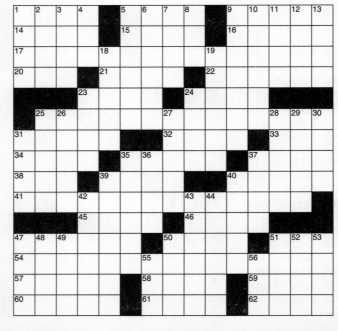

91 ORDINALITY

by Shirley Soloway

ACROSS

1 Fabric surface
5 Kansas Indian
10 Bad reviews
14 Smell __ (be suspicious)
15 ALF or Mork
16 Touched down
17 "To begin with . . ."
20 Youngsters
21 Falk or Boyle
22 Hem or baste
23 Resident's suffix
25 Spanish river
27 Infielder
34 Antiquity
35 Studied, with "over"
36 The __ Lama
38 Bridle strap
40 Alabama city
42 Air strike
43 Change prices
45 States with conviction
47 Campers' vehicles, for short
48 Tune from a Welles film, with "The"
51 Romanian money
52 Sweet potato
53 Seer's gift: Abbr.
56 Sport shoe attachment
60 Ethical
64 Reporters
67 Banned act
68 Mythical giant
69 Author Hunter
70 Not home
71 Trial races
72 Singer Coolidge

DOWN

1 Bide one's time
2 British composer Thomas __
3 Past due
4 Racial
5 Clumsy one
6 Blunder
7 Suffix for million
8 Adventure tale
9 Comes in
10 Buddy
11 "Woe is me!"
12 Pleasant
13 Cook slowly
18 Prevent legally
19 Was nosy
24 Slaughter of baseball
26 Sharif of *Funny Girl*
27 Icy rain
28 Mrs. Bunker
29 Wild fancy
30 Writer Plain
31 Promo producers
32 Warning sound
33 Ingenuous
34 Go awry
37 Psyche parts
39 Hit precisely
41 Pretentious
44 Painter El __
46 Pillow covers
49 Minnesota city
50 Overactor
53 Italian volcano
54 Display
55 Clinton cabinet member
57 New York canal
58 "__ boy!"
59 One of those
61 Sitarist Shankar
62 Rat-__
63 Horne or Olin
65 Vaudevillian Eddie
66 Naval off.

TUTTI-FRUTTI

by Fred Piscop

ACROSS

1 Roman robes
6 Muddy
10 *What's My Line?* regular
14 Make excuses
15 Bread spread
16 A Great Lake
17 Single-export countries
20 Aerial sighting
21 Garden flower, for short
22 Periodic-table stats.
23 Phone inventor
24 Cartoon bear
26 Seafood selection
33 Distinctive quality
34 Russian sea
35 Wrath
36 "__ the Mood for Love"
37 Grow toward morning
39 Seth's brother
40 Mythical bird
41 English river
42 Sandberg of baseball
43 South African province
48 Wraps up
49 Golf gadgets
50 Hurler Satchel
53 Composer Bartók
54 Ring ref's call
57 Hair color
61 ERA or RBI
62 Actor Richard
63 Like some seals
64 __ out (ignore)
65 Network junction
66 Has a feast

DOWN

1 Prohibition
2 Norwegian monarch
3 Singer Vannelli
4 Attorneys' org.
5 Big name in sewing
6 Principals
7 __ *Three Lives*
8 Sen.'s counterpart
9 __ *Are There*
10 Boston hoopster
11 Actress Gray
12 Puerto __
13 Actor Parker
18 Comrade
19 Breakfast selection
23 Breakfast selection
24 Long ago
25 __ upswing (rising)
26 Port on the Nile
27 Wit
28 Novelist Jong
29 Spud
30 Benghazi's land
31 Don't exist
32 Donnybrook
37 Fibbed
38 Kennel comments
39 Word after fine or liberal
41 Nixon's first veep
44 Bring to naught
45 Everlasting, old-style
46 Slithery
47 Ocean floor
50 "Hey, you!"
51 Aleutian island
52 Armenia neighbor
53 Actor Pitt
54 Ripped
55 It's above the shin
56 Two to one, e.g.
58 Golfing great Hogan
59 Self-importance
60 Chou En-__

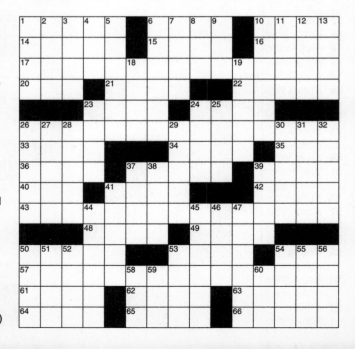

93 BARBERISM

by Bob Lubbers

ACROSS

1 Sandwich meat
5 Most contemptible
11 Tam or beret
14 "I cannot tell __"
15 Fatty ester
16 Be in debt
17 Nothing: Sp.
18 Postpones
19 Allow
20 Staunch
23 Diarist Ned
24 __ cri (hot fashion)
27 Ques. response
28 To be: Fr.
32 Hawkins of Dogpatch
33 "Oh, no!" to José
36 Actress Rowlands
37 Like a hive
39 Qatar money
41 Have empathy toward
42 Part of French Indochina
44 Shade trees
45 Equip with guns
48 Fashion zealot
51 Word form for "bone"
53 Separated
57 Actor Wallach
59 Pre-cable need
60 Comic Johnson
61 Legendary bird
62 Actor Depardieu
63 Stadium level
64 Inquire
65 Rubs off
66 Latvia and Lithuania, once: Abbr.

DOWN

1 Dee or Bullock
2 __ words (pun)
3 Helpers
4 Union general
5 Petty officer, for short
6 Landed
7 Clockmaker Thomas
8 Grew less tense
9 Vermont ski center
10 Domingo and Carreras
11 Met head-on
12 Reverence
13 Cat or dog
21 "What __ to say is . . ."
22 Wild donkey
25 German article
26 Actor Stephen
29 Not kosher
30 Actress Martha
31 Jay Leno, e.g.
33 Piña __ (rum drink)
34 Cottonseed pod
35 Like some radios: Abbr.
37 Choose selectively
38 Close, as friends
39 Eng. fliers
40 "__ pig's eye!"
43 Desert "sight"
45 Video-game systems
46 Leaseholder
47 Bill of PBS
49 Range beast
50 __ firma
52 Small fights
54 "Buenos __" (good morning: Sp.)
55 Give a hoot
56 Car pioneer
57 Historical period
58 __ Alamos, NM

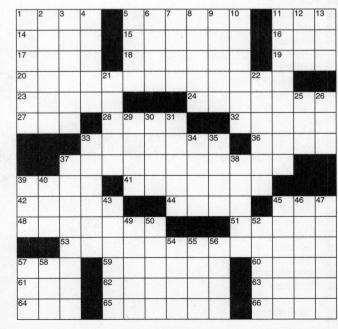

by Randy Sowell

ACROSS

1 "Thanks __!"
5 Beseech
9 Nebraska city
14 Stun
15 Beans partner
16 Legitimate
17 Clarinet cousin
18 Lamb's pseudonym
19 Sharp
20 Florida beach
23 "I'll say!"
24 Like steppes
25 Big __, CA
27 __ Tin Tin
28 1987 sci-fi film
32 Barbecue residue
35 Dorothy's dog
38 __ Gay (WWII plane)
39 War of 1898
43 Kitchen plastic
44 Part of a list
45 Industrious insect
46 Golfer Lee
48 Corn portion
51 "Am __ understand that . . ."
52 Senator Warner's state
57 Eager
60 Connecticut city
62 __ Open (PGA stop)
64 "Zip-__-Doo-Dah"
65 Fencer's need
66 Type size
67 Connery of The Rock

68 Without: Fr.
69 Garden pests
70 Romance novelist Victoria
71 Waste allowance

DOWN

1 Choose to use
2 Cabinet department
3 Form of oxygen
4 Wobble
5 Forestalls
6 Makes angry
7 Etcher's needs
8 Calendar span
9 Eggs: Lat.

10 Pasta
11 Graduate, for short
12 Author Shere
13 Yemeni port
21 Inventor Whitney
22 Words from Chan
26 Over: Ger.
28 Apple variety
29 Caesar's TV partner
30 The Good Earth heroine
31 Gasp
32 Aide: Abbr.
33 Practice boxing
34 Fabled racer
36 The Buckeye State

37 Make lace
40 Steer the ship
41 Monogram part: Abbr.
42 Rising
47 San Francisco hill
49 Mature
50 Most mature
52 MTV offering
53 Perfect
54 Kind of stock
55 Papas or Dunne
56 Bikini blast
57 Alan Arkin's son
58 Enthusiastic
59 Reverend Roberts
61 Hasty
63 __ Misérables

95 SMALL CHANGE

by Shannon Burns

ACROSS

1 Hotelier Helmsley
6 Church platform
11 Egyptian snake
14 Bandleader Desi
15 Baby grand, e.g.
16 Gambler's cube
17 Considerable amount of money
19 "How was __ know?"
20 Slippery swimmers
21 Capital of Jordan
23 Handcuff
27 Assistants
29 Beast
30 Lifestyle writer Stewart
31 Military survey, for short
32 Brief incursion
33 i topper
36 Printer's needs
37 Assigns a value to
38 Got up
39 Keats creation
40 Jaguar and Cougar
41 Hair cutter
42 Moon vehicle
44 Flattens out
45 Scrubbed a mission
47 Award hopeful
48 Wheel spokes
49 Frat party garb
50 Wrath
51 Football VIP
58 In the past

59 Word before berth or class
60 __ eleison (Mass section)
61 Trent Lott, e.g.: Abbr.
62 Lauder of perfumes
63 Dilapidated

DOWN

1 Drink like a cat
2 Make mistakes
3 Singleton
4 __ King Cole
5 Pertaining to Montezuma's people
6 Pie fruit
7 "My Bonnie __ over . . ."
8 Catch some rays
9 Landers or Miller
10 Privileged class
11 Very common
12 Instrument for 38 Down
13 Menial workers
18 Holler
22 Speedometer abbr.
23 Cuomo or Puzo
24 Put __ to (stop)
25 Kids' cable-TV network
26 Andy's radio pal
27 Rabbits' kin
28 Historical periods
30 Engine
32 Destined

34 "__ Mio"
35 Short in speech
37 None too polite
38 Musician Shankar
40 Old item
41 Comments
43 Exodus hero
44 Theater box
45 Operatic solos
46 Harbor craft
47 The Hunchback of __ Dame
49 Spruce or maple
52 FedEx rival
53 Likely
54 "See ya!"
55 "__ we there yet?"
56 El __ (Spanish hero)
57 Door opener

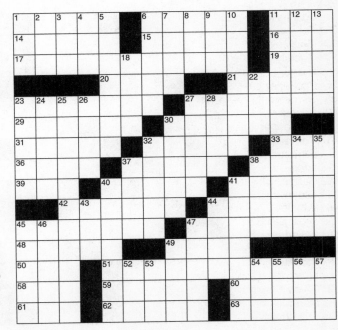

ACROSS

1 Inventory entry
5 Gym pad
8 Buccaneers' home
13 Oscar __ Renta
14 Store sign
15 Studio sign
16 Gives up
18 Stickum
19 Waiter's burden
20 Discharges
21 What a glance sometimes does
25 Perpetual, old-style
26 Muscat native
27 Quemoy neighbor
28 Narrow opening
29 Fellow
33 Goof
34 Ghostly image
37 Pitcher's stat
38 GI hangouts
40 Actress Gardner et al.
41 Computer correspond- ence
43 German city
45 Slip away
46 Babbles
49 Journalist Bly
50 Palindromic name
51 Famous furrier
52 Gives a false alarm
57 Pub staple
58 American Beauty, e.g.
59 Region
60 Aides: Abbr.
61 Lyric poem
62 Monthly payment

DOWN

1 Driver's licenses, e.g.: Abbr.
2 Afternoon drink
3 TV Tarzan
4 High achievers
5 Thanksgiving Day parade sponsor
6 Totally
7 Golf gizmo
8 Cruise film of '86
9 Listless, in London
10 En __ (together)
11 Actress Zasu
12 War god
14 Asp, for one
17 Neptune neighbor
20 Gladden
21 Sky sights
22 Word form for "rock"
23 Lava spewer
24 Leaves out
25 Winged walker
28 Lucky number
30 Mounds
31 Come up
32 Wan
35 Out of style
36 Rents again
39 SRO show
42 Legendary racehorse
44 Avoids
45 Cosmetician Lauder
46 Trials
47 Choir voices
48 Harsh sound
49 Shuttle grp.
52 __-Magnon
53 Angler's need
54 Mine load
55 Dawson or Deighton
56 Skim milk's lack

ACROSS

1 Young girls
6 Desist
11 Hit on the head
14 Parcel out
15 Aides: Abbr.
16 Yoko __
17 Uncontestable
19 Actor Kingsley
20 Novelist Bagnold
21 Green stone
23 Fidel's ally
25 Greek letters
27 Ball-__ hammer
28 __-mo replay
29 Nudge
31 1506, to Caesar
34 Magical drink
36 Part of a nation's military might
38 Names of some tsars
39 Goods-and-services meas.
40 __ barrel (lacking choice)
41 Melted down
43 Chicken part
44 Word form for "within"
45 Political refugee
47 Collar shape
48 Farm tools
50 Teachers' org.
51 Koppel or Knight
52 Be manager of

55 Queue
57 Meadow
58 Compromise
63 State leader: Abbr.
64 Happening
65 Knight wear
66 Whichever
67 Richards of tennis
68 Key letter

DOWN

1 __ Tse-tung
2 European mountain
3 __ de France
4 Gift recipient
5 Getz or Kenton
6 Woolen braid
7 Double curve

8 Arthur of tennis
9 Tough puzzle
10 Lauder of cosmetics
11 Box defensively
12 Like Nash's lama
13 Small body of water
18 37th President
22 Eliminate
23 Split, as a hoof
24 Torridly
26 Actor's sub
28 Church topper
29 Ferrer or Greco
30 Rim

32 Well-__ (adept)
33 Quite angry
35 Not alfresco
37 Skin opening
39 Jewel
42 Fidgety
43 Egghead
46 Become more solid
49 Gung-ho
51 Neon fish
52 Olympian Korbut
53 Laborer
54 Tied
56 Bismarck's loc.
59 Wind dir.
60 Current unit
61 Keystone comic
62 Memorable time

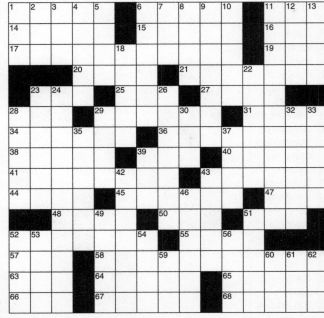

98 EXTREMITIES

by Rich Norris

ACROSS

1 Religious group
5 Legend maker
10 "__ girl!"
14 Actress __ Flynn Boyle
15 Kept going
16 Sink alternative
17 Fair
19 Got up
20 Game for a tot
21 Encountering great difficulty
23 "Too bad!"
24 Party offering
25 Onassis, familiarly
26 __ in Terris (papal encyclical)
28 Lord Peter of whodunits
31 Namely
34 Of an orbital intersection
36 Three: It.
37 Word of assent
38 Reveal
39 Ward of *Sisters*
40 Brewed drink
41 Make ready anew, as a ship
42 Computer programmer
43 Low joints
45 Main concern
47 Mauna __
48 TV superstation
49 Draft org.
52 Calgary's country
55 Boundless
57 Finished
58 Like mountain goats
60 Bearing
61 Burning up
62 Ore source
63 Probability
64 Marshal's group
65 __ about (legal phrase)

DOWN

1 Took a nap
2 Roof overhangs
3 Small stream
4 Army vehicle
5 Semitic language
6 Kitchen tool
7 Take apart
8 Fish eggs
9 *The King* __
10 Teeming
11 Macho
12 *Kon-*__
13 NYSE counterpart
18 Went after
22 Fingertip cover
26 Brooch, e.g.
27 Dominant theme
28 Pale
29 First name in mysteries
30 Fiscal period
31 "Bye!"
32 Sign of the future
33 Irresolute
35 Morning walkers
38 Bandleader Brown
39 Maritime signal
41 Peruse
42 Novelty
44 Finds out
46 Morning quaff
49 Kind of protest
50 Pool employee of old
51 Passover ritual
52 "It's Impossible" singer
53 Enthusiastic
54 Kin of PDQ
55 Eye part
56 Dodger pitcher Hideo
59 *X-Files* topic

99 IN THE CARDS

by Lee Weaver

ACROSS

1 Unclad
5 Burn a bit
9 Kentucky resource
13 Son of Adam
14 Routine task
15 Forearm bone
16 Go away
18 Take care of
19 Dawn goddess
20 Western marshal of note
21 Inedible oranges
23 Fanciful visions
25 Carpenter's need
27 Ballpark officials
29 Pierces
33 Squander
36 Top-notch
38 Small sailing vessel
39 Sandwich cookie
40 More cunning
41 Algonquian language
42 Donna or Rex
43 Still
44 Room and __
45 Portuguese wine
47 On the briny
49 Second president
51 Short snooze
55 Ski race
58 Scent
60 Balin or Claire
61 Isolated
62 Lower levels, on a ship
65 Ripening agent
66 Carpenter's need
67 Animal skin
68 Knocks for a loop
69 Makes do, with "out"
70 Son of Hera

DOWN

1 Stationed
2 Really detest
3 Exploit again
4 Santa's helper
5 Sonny's ex
6 Basketball targets
7 Canine comment
8 Carry Nation, e.g.
9 Gentleman's formal attire
10 Couturier Cassini
11 Queen Elizabeth's daughter
12 Youngsters
14 Necklace fastening
17 __ fatale
22 Aug. follower
24 Sedan sellers
26 Movies
28 Low bow
30 Zhivago's beloved
31 Water pitcher
32 Luge or toboggan
33 NIghtcrawler
34 Field of study
35 Plant-to-be
37 Popeye's Olive
40 Mix up
44 Chef James
46 Wedding promise
48 Threatening look
50 Puzzle out
52 More pleasant
53 Place for a bracelet
54 Subjects of memoirs
55 Deli purchase
56 Company emblem
57 All over again
59 Deer mothers
63 Cartoon exclamation
64 Antipollution agcy.

by Bob Lubbers

ACROSS

1 German river
5 Fresh talk
9 Anatomical partitions
14 Cairo's river
15 Author Wiesel
16 Enter
17 Health
19 One at __ (singly)
20 Makes use (of)
21 Scams
23 Practice
25 New York canal
26 Proofreader's mark
27 Allegiance
29 Actor Ray
32 Precludes
34 __ *Got a Secret*
36 Overcooked
38 Consume
39 Mesopotamia region
41 Wind dir.
42 Submit, as homework
45 Legendary loch
46 Evaluate
48 Fem. opposite
50 "__ it!" ("Amen!")
51 Bucolic
55 Say an "h"
58 Kodak product
59 Leighton of *Melrose Place*
60 Stationery imprint
62 French weapons
63 Religious image
64 Western Indian
65 Scruffs
66 Lady's man
67 Slangy noes

DOWN

1 "First __, first . . ."
2 Strainer
3 Islam's Almighty
4 Needs, in a way
5 Is angry
6 Baba or MacGraw
7 Subsequently
8 Utah lily
9 Manatee meal
10 Involve
11 Broadcasting period
12 Voluminous work
13 Pub servings
18 Raucous noise
22 __-do-well
24 Some Dutch paintings
27 Daughter of Muhammad
28 Actor Montand
29 Lincoln's nickname
30 Moon goddess
31 Fancy shoe
33 Naughty
35 Hesitation sounds
37 Pentagon VIPs
40 Rare
43 Cruising
44 Newborn
47 Evening party
49 Polaris, e.g.
51 Tranquillity
52 Lasso
53 Vane pointer
54 Huron and Mead
55 Admiral Shepard
56 Gilbert of *Roseanne*
57 Small branch
61 Heavy weight

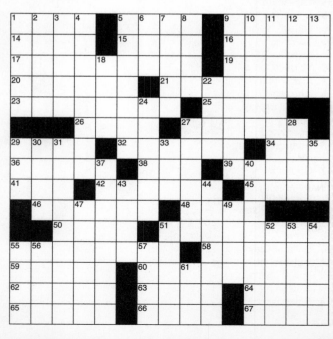

But wait. . . there's more!

Now that you're done with this book, we invite you to select your next book from the complete Random House Puzzles & Games catalog — which has nearly 200 uniquely diverse puzzle books for you to choose from!

These include America's most respected names in puzzledom:

- **The New York Times**
- **The Boston Globe**
- **New York Magazine**
- **Random House**
- **The Washington Post**
- **Los Angeles Times**
- **Games Magazine**

And you'll also find these:

Acrostics
Cryptic Crosswords
Large Print Crosswords
New York TImes Crossword Reference Books
Extra-Value Collections (with up to 1,000 puzzles per book!)

To get your free catalog (plus a **FREE** puzzle),
please call us toll-free (weekdays 9 A.M. to 5 P.M.):

1-800-793-2665

and ask for your free "Random House Puzzle Catalog."

Or clip and mail the coupon below.

To: Random House Puzzles & Games, P.O. Box 750
    Massapequa Park, New York 11762

NAME (please print)

ADDRESS

CITY   STATE   ZIP

E-MAIL ADDRESS

ANSWERS

1

```
ATTU  STAR  EMBED
REIN  TOPE  MAUNA
ALES  RUED  PILED
BLUEBERRYHILL
 APART  SEER  FRI
  TACS   DEARER
JAM  CHERRYSTONE
ALID  ROO   AGES
DATEOFBIRTH  SET
EMILIO    YEAR
DOG  LIPS  EROSE
 APPLECOMPUTER
MITLA  DALI  TARA
OCEAN  ALAN  EGIS
PESTS  LANG  DEEP
```

2

```
SEGAL  REPEL  TAD
OCOME  ADALE  ARE
WHOSONFIRST   III
SOD  PATES  MONET
  NOAMS   DEFTLY
EMIGRE   TARIFF
RAGED  VIXEN  USE
ACHE  DICED  SNAG
SET  BUNKS  SANTA
 GLADES  SPAYED
ACROSS   SWARM
CHATS  OSCAR  CSA
TIC  EDGARBERGEN
ELI  TULSA  STEED
DIE  SHEEP  TEEMS
```

3

```
DUAL   SHOOT  LEAK
INNO   ROLFE  OGRE
STICKSHIFT   GILA
TITAN  ONT  HASON
SEALAB   SOLAR
   VAT   ALIAS
LIMBERUP   TOTTER
EVER  KEACH  HOWE
SESAME   STEMMING
SANER   SRI
  CASTS   SNATCH
STAHL  REA   ITALO
TONO  MATCHMAKER
ALOU  ADATE  LEAD
BENT  BETSY  ERTE
```

4

```
ABBE   TODDS  HUSH
BORN   AWAIT  ONTO
ROADRUNNER   ADAS
ANTEUP   EMERGENT
  ALEC    WEIR
SURE  ANO   VETCH
AONE  APERCU  ARE
WOODYWOODPECKER
LTR   PENNER  HEWS
SHIER  SSA   MASS
  GAEL   LAIR
SCISSORS   BLADES
LONI  DONALDDUCK
URAL  ELOPE  ESTE
RELY  SEWER  STOW
```

5

```
ABBY   CHAP   GRAFT
LOLA   HULA   EARLE
IHOP   AGER   OILER
SEW  KNOCKEDDOWN
TABBIES    JUS
  YELL  SPEC   PAC
PABLO  CHOCKFULL
OSLO   THANT  ONTO
SHOWERING   MCCOY
HEW  DONE   YEAH
  TWO   SEALERS
TAKEAPOKEAT   DOW
AREAR  DANG   MOUE
SNERD  ELSE   RUSE
SONYS  SEER   STEP
```

6

```
SKATE    BOER   OPS
INDEX   HORNE   RAT
BEATTHEODDS    APE
SER  OARS    ECLAT
 DEARIE  DANA
   STRIKEITRICH
 TAPE   NED   POLA
NADIR  BUD   CANAL
AUER   SAT    ORAN
BREAKTHEBANK
   TOES   OPTSTO
BORES    JOSE   AFT
EVE  HITANEXACTA
TEN  ERODE  TAKER
ART  RATE   SAYNO
```

7

```
GRIMM  TWAS   SCOT
RODEO  HELP   PACE
AGENT  ELLA   ARES
PEASHOOTERS    RAT
HRS   END  NEWTONS
  RIOT    DART
HAHA  ORE   PATIO
ATOP  NERVE  PORE
LATHE  MER   SPAR
 PIPS   SHAH
ERODING  ITO  DAB
VAT  CORNCOBPIPE
ADAM  REAL   BEARS
NITA  EAVE   ERNIE
SOOT  RTES   SMELT
```

8

```
MAJOR  SPF   DIET
AWARE  TOLD   EDGY
MOWED  ALAI   LEON
ALB  ELBOWGREASE
 RHEAS     EAT
STEAMY    DISKETTE
ORALS   FORTE   URN
LAKE   COVES  GRIT
ICE   OARED  BETTE
DERRICKS   SEALER
 ELK    SHARE
KNEESLAPPER   NIT
EARL   ELIA   CREDO
NILE   DINT   UNCLE
SLED   TEE   BAKES
```

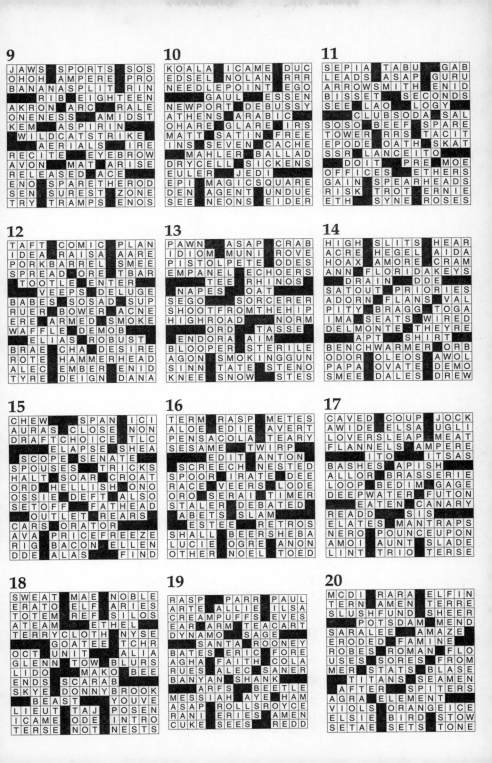

9

```
JAWS_SPORTS__SOS
OHOH_AMPERE__PRO
BANANASPLIT__RIN
___RIB__EIGHTEEN
AKRON_ARC__RALE_
ONENESS__AMIDST_
KEM___ASPIRIN___
_WILDCATSTRIKE__
___AERIALS___IRE
_RECITE__EYEBROW
AVON__MAT__ARISE
RELEASED__ACE___
ENO_SPARETHEROD_
SEN_SUREST__ZONE
TRY_TRAMPS__ENOS
```

10

```
KOALA_ICAME__DUC
EDSEL_NOLAN__RRR
NEEDLEPOINT__EGO
____GAUL___ESSEN
NEWPORT__DEBUSSY
ATHENS__ARABIC__
OHARE__GLARE_IRS
MATT__SATIN_FREE
INS__SEVEN_CACHE
__MAHLER__BALLAD
DRYCELL__SICKENS
EULER__JEDI_____
EPI_MAGICSQUARE_
DEN_AGENT__UNDUE
SEE_NEONS__EIDER
```

11

```
SEPIA_TABU__GAB_
LEADS_ASAP__GURU
ARROWSMITH__ENID
BISSET__SECONDS_
SEE__LAO__LOGY__
__CLUBSODA__SAL_
SOSO_BEEF__SPARE
TOWER_RRS__TACIT
EPODE_OATH__SKAT
SSR__LANCEITO___
_DOIT__PRE__MOE_
OFFICES__ETHERS_
GAIN_SPEARHEADS_
RISK_TROT__ERNIE
ETH__SYNE__ROSES
```

12

```
TAFT_COMIC__PLAN
IDEA_RAISA__AARE
PORKBARREL__SMEE
SPREAD_ORE__TBAR
_TOOTLE_ENTER___
_VEEPS__DELUGE__
BABES_SOSAD__SUP
RUER_BOWER__ACNE
ERE_ARMED__SMOKE
WAFFLE__DEMOB___
_ELIAS__ROBUST__
BRAE_CHA__DESIRE
ROTE_HAMMERHEAD_
ALEC_EMBER__ENID
TYRE_DEIGN__DANA
```

13

```
PAWN__ASAP__CRAB
IDIOM_MUNI__ROVE
PISTOLPETE__ODES
EMPANEL__ECHOERS
___TEE__RHINOS__
NAPES___OAT_____
SEGO__SORCERER__
SHOOTFROMTHEHIP_
HIGHROAD__NORM__
_____ORD__TASSE_
ENDORA___AIM____
BLOOPER__STERILE
AGON_SMOKINGGUN_
SINN_TATE__STENO
KNEE_SNOW__STES_
```

14

```
HIGH_SLITS__HEAR
ACRE_HEGEL__AIDA
HOAX_AMORE__CRAM
ANN_FLORIDAKEYS_
___DRAIN___DDE__
SATOUT__PRIORIES
ADORN_FLANS__VAL
PITY_BRAGG__TOGA
IMA_SEATS__WIRED
DELMONTE__THEYRE
___APT__SHIRT___
BENCHWARMER__ORB
ODOR_OLEOS__AWOL
PAPA_OVATE__DEMO
SMEE_DALES__DREW
```

15

```
CHEW___SPAN__ICI
AURAS_CLOSE__NON
DRAFTCHOICE__TLC
__ELAPSE___SHEA_
_SCOPE__SENATE__
SPOUSES__TRICKS_
HALT_SOAR__CROAT
ORD_HELLISH__ONO
OSSIE_DEFT__ALSO
SETOFF__FATHEAD_
_OUTLET__REARS__
CARS__ORATOR____
AVA_PRICEFREEZE_
RIG_BACON__ELLEN
DDE_ALAS____FIND
```

16

```
TERM_RASP__METES
ALOE_EDIE__AVERT
PENSACOLA__TEARY
SESAME___TWIRP__
____EDIT__ANTON_
SCREECH__NESTED_
SPOOR_IRATE__DEE
RACE_VEERS__LODE
ORO_SERAI__TIMER
STALER__DEBATED_
_ABETS__SLAM____
_ESTEE___RETROS_
SHALL_BEERSHEBA_
LUCIE_OGRE__ANON
OTHER_NOEL__TOED
```

17

```
CAVED_COUP__JOCK
AWIDE_ELSA__UGLI
LOVERSLEAP__MEAT
FLANNELS__AMPERE
___ITO____ITSAS_
BASHES___APISH__
ALLOR__BRASSERIE
LOOP_BEDIM__GAGE
DEEPWATER__FUTON
__EATEN__CANARY_
READD____SIS____
ELATES__MANTRAPS
NERO_POUNCEUPON_
AMOI_AUNT__SLADE
LINT_TRIO__TERSE
```

18

```
SWEAT__MAE__NOBLE
ERATO_ELF__ARIES
TOTEM_REF__SILOS
ATEAM____ETHEL__
TERRYCLOTH__NYSE
_GOATEE___TCHR__
OCT_UNIT___ALIA_
GLENN_TOW__BLURS
LIDO_MAKO___BEE_
ENDS__SCARAB____
SKYE_DONNYBROOK_
_BEAST____YOUVE_
LIEUT_TAJ__POSEN
ICAME_ODE__INTRO
TERSE_NOT__NESTS
```

19

```
RASP__PARR__PAUL
ARTE_ALLIE__ILSA
CREAMPUFFS__EVES
EAR_ARM__TEACART
DYNAMO___SAGE___
___SANTA__ROONEY
BATES_ERIC__FORE
AGHA_FAITH__COLA
RUES_ALEC__SANER
BANYAN__SHANK___
_ARFS___BEETLE__
MESSIAH_AYE__HAM
ASAP_ROLLSROYCE_
RANI_ERIES__AMEN
CUKE_SEES___REDD
```

20

```
MCDI_RARA__ELFIN
TERN_AMEN__TERRE
SLUSHFUND__SHEER
___POTSDAM__MEND
SARALEE__AMAZE__
ERODED__FAMINE__
ROBES_ROMAN__FLO
USES_SORES__FROM
MER_STATS__BLASE
_TITANS__SEAMEN_
AFTER___SPITERS_
AGRA__ELEMENT___
VIOLS_ORANGEICE_
ELSIE_BIRD__STOW
SETAE_SETS__TONE
```

21

```
O M A H A   R E F S   S A M
L O L A S   F E E L A   P L O
D E E D S   A N N U L   A I R
  J E R S E Y B O U N C E
A S P   S O T S   D O N K E Y
C L A S S A     F U N D
C O T T O N C L U B   R A N I
T O T E R   H O N   H E L E N
S P I N   H I T T H E S I L K
    C R O P   O N S A L E
A R T I E R   W R A P   S Y R
W O O L G A T H E R E D
A D O   A T R I A   C R U S T
K I T   R I O T S   K A T I E
E N S   D O T E   S T E R N
```

22

```
B L O B   C H E F S   B R A T
I A G O   R O S I E   L I V E
O S L O   A M A N A   A M E N
S H E M   B O U N C E B A C K
    E M B   S O L
S M A R T E D   A M B I T
L A M A S   R A T S   U P O N
A M I N   L I C I T   N A M E
W I N G   O P E N   A G N E S
E O S I N   A B R E A S T
    T E L   R T E
F I R S T S E R V E   C H I C
A B I E   T A H O E   O A T H
L E S T   A V O I D   R H E A
A X E S   R E S T S   D A M P
```

23

```
S T A T   B O M B   P I C K S
P O L A   O R A L   O W L E T
I R O N H O R S E   W E E N Y
N O U G A T   C A M E R A
      R I A   T A L E N T S
S E D A T E L Y   C L A S S A
I N U S E   L A C E S   W E S
T A S K   L O W E S   G E T S
A M T   S E W E D   R E E S E
R E J E C T   D E C A M P E D
S L A L O M S   S U N
  C A R E E R   R E A T A S
A R K I N   W H I T E W A S H
S C E N E   E E L S   E R I E
S A T E D   R E L Y   D A N S
```

24

```
M A C H   R U C K S   Z A G
E C H O   O Z Z I E   M E T O
T R A M   D I A N A   I L E D
S E R E N E   R E M E D I A L
  O B O L     A N G R Y
G R A N A D A   A C T I
L E S T   R U M B A   G R E W
O A T H   I D I O T   H O L E
B R I E   V E L D T   T O L L
  R U E D   E L E C T E D
D E C A F     S E R O
E C O N O M I C   C A W I N G
S L A G   O M A H A   B R I O
K A T E   B A N A L   O A T S
S T S   S M E L L   Y E A H
```

25

```
L E E R   M U N C H   O B O E
I D L E   O P E R A   B R I G
S I L V E R S T A R   T A N G
T E A S E R   L T D   A S K S
    R O S I E   H I S
E D G E   W O K   M A N T R A
L I O N S   B E G A T   A I L
O N L E A V E   R E C Y C L E
P E D   M A R C O   H I K E R
E D I S O N   A P R   P S S T
    E T A   S T E E P
H A H A   S T S   S E A N C E
O V A L   C O P P E R H E A D
B O W L   A V A I L   A R I D
O W N S   N E W E L   B O N Y
```

26

```
N E O N   R E A M   L I M O
E T R E   P E N T A G O N A L
W E E W I L L I E W I N K I E
    T R E A D E R S   S L O
L E D   K A T   T R I E S
B L E W   S E R F S   E N D
J A M E S     O L L I E
L I T T L E B O Y B L U E
  B U E N O     N E L L S
D M A   O A T H S   D A L I
L E A R N   A K A   N A T
I F I   I M M A T U R E
T I N Y T I M C R A T C H I T
R E S E A R C H E S   H A R E
E S T A   V I E D   O M E N
```

27

```
  C A N E   C O M B   E Y E S
A L G O L   O R C A   S E L A
P U R P L E R A I N   C L A N
B E E L I N E   I S A   L T D
  S E A S T A R   H A L O E S
    C O O   H E E H A W
L E B E N   L Y L E   T S A R
A L L   B A T E S   E P A
G L U E   A C H E   S W A R M
  E P O N Y M   H E H
R E B I N D   S O O T I E R
A R A   E A R   G L I M M E R
M A Y S   G O L D E N P O N D
I T O N   E L I E   T E T E S
S O U L   S E E N   O R E S
```

28

```
D E W E Y   G A S P   E L L
O C H R E   A L T A R   D I A
T H I N S   R E A T A   N A M
S O T   O L D G R A Y M A R E
    E E R I E   C O O
A T H A N D   P I A N I S T
P H O T O   Y A N K S   A I R
E R R S   B E R N E   A M M O
S O S   G I L E S   B L U E R
B E F A L L S   L I V E R Y
    A M O   S E G A L
P O N Y E X P R E S S   C S A
I I I   T I E O N   H O O T S
A S K   E A S E S   O L L I E
F E E   N O S E   T E T R A
```

29

```
P A C T   A G A R   P E C A N
E M I L   M E S A   A T O N E
W A T C H O N T H E R H I N E
S T Y   A U R A   L E A F E D
    F I N E   C O N N
A S S E R T   R A P T   E E N
S T A N D   G A M E   A C L U
S Y N C O P A T E D C L O C K
A R T E   A B E L   A L L I E
M O O   F R E D   S P E E D S
    T I C S   A H O Y
S I M O N E   E L A N   P A D
H O U R G L A S S F I G U R E
A T I M E   S P O T   A M E N
D A R E R   H O P S   S P A T
```

30

```
S T E P   R I D D   C H A K A
P A R E   O D O R   H U M A N
E M M A   B A N A N A B O A T
A P A C H E   A M A S   S T E
R A S H E R S   A S T O
    B A T O N   S E R A P E
A P A R T   N A M E   A G A L
L I N A   S A V O R   N E T S
E T O N   T R A P   A G R E E
C A N D L E   L E D G E
    Y E A R   D R E S S E R
A S P   A M O R   A S T U T E
C H E R R Y B O M B   I S A N
H E R O N   E M I L   C A P E
E D I C T   D E N Y   K N E E
```

31

```
Z I P S   M I L E S   C A T S
U T E P   A D E A L   A L I E
L E N A   T E A S E   N I N E
U R N   Q U A R T E R D E C K
  Y O U R S   P O I N T S
S W A N E E   S T E E D
T E N S E   A P E R   E D A M
A R T   N O S I E S T   I V E
R E E D   V E L D   A D M I T
  I D E A L   C L E E S E
G R O C E R   T H O R N
N I C K E L O D E O N   O F F
O G E E   A D A N O   E V I L
M O A N   N I N O S   N E V A
E R N S   D E E R E   S L E W
```

32

```
H A Z E D   S P A S   C A R D
E L O P E   C O O K   A L O U
S O N I C   A N N E   N E A T
S P E C I A L D E L I V E R Y
      D I P   E R A
H A L T E R   A T T E S T S
O L E O   O L E A N   U P A
S I N G I N G T E L E G R A M
E M T   S A L O N   A N T I
  B O W T I E S   B O S S E D
      A L L   S A R
S E A L E D W I T H A K I S S
T U R K   O R N O   N E O N S
A R I E   W A R P   G E T I T
B O A R   N Y E S   S P A T S
```

33

```
SEA   PASSE TALES
ANT   ALIEN ARENA
ITO   PALED CAGES
PINTAILDUCK   AMS
AREAS     ROY  TIE
NEST  DARED PIER
    AERO  CROSS
  PANICBUTTON
AHARD   IKES
CENT  ANNEX  DATA
CRO   UNE    MESAS
OER   SNAPTHEWHIP
STATE RUMOR  OLE
TIMOR EMEER  RON
SCAMS DANDY  ERS
```

34

```
GUARE  SASH  BIBI
ANNEX  POLE  UBER
STAMP  ONOR  RENO
PIT  LAKEWOBEGON
SLO    ORE    IRA
  MADISONCOUNTY
WHILED LESS  EOE
HAZY   UDO   AGRA
OWE  EASE  MAILER
  ANDERSONVILLE
IOU    IST   CPA
PEYTONPLACE  TOP
UTAH  DOIN  RAIDS
MULE  EKED  ERNIE
PIER  REDS  DEGAS
```

35

```
LAGS  ODESSA  BAN
ECRU  PANTED  EVE
CHICKENFEED   EER
HYPHEN  LAM   AFRO
     NEPAL    OLE
ROPE   ROM  CABANA
ABOVE  SEEDS  TAG
DERANGE  TRIREME
ASK   TORCH  SIREN
REPORT  LEE   PSST
   ICY   CALLA
ABET   SOY  ARTIST
BAH   MUTTONCHOPS
BRA   RETOLD  ATOP
EDT   STANDS  TATS
```

36

```
PASSE  GARTH   SPA
ASPEN  ALOHA   TAC
SPIRALSTAIRCASE
HIRE   PLANNER
ARI  ASI   SIFTS
SETON  TAME   TAKE
   UNO  RELATION
  STEPMONSTER
BRUSSELS   ERR
BART   DIET  ISLES
SHERE   AGA   ALT
  IMITATE   INDO
CORPORATELADDER
ARK   TIMER  MEESE
BOO   ESSES  PARTS
```

37

```
NURMI  ATRIP   APO
ONEAL  DIANA   DAG
VINYLSIDING   LIL
ATTA   TEAS  OSAGE
  FOULARDTIES
FASCIA      HAI
ALLAN  ROUE  MIST
ROUNDHOUSEPUNCH
MEGA   ANTE  ALTAI
    SAT   ELIOTS
  SWITCHBLADE
CARAT  RANI   SASS
AGE   SOUNDTRACKS
LEN   INNER  ADMIT
ERE   NOOSE  MEETS
```

38

```
PAMPA  HERS   RATS
AMAIN  ABEL   OMIT
DINGY  HOPI   MOMA
SDI   PIANOPLAYER
   CLODS    SON
RUERS   ETHIOPIA
WORST  CARON   ISL
EGIS   SHRED  OCTO
BUS   ATALE  ANKLE
SETTLERS   DRUPE
   OER   FIRPO
GOLDENGLOVE   CPU
IRED   ELAL  SAKES
SEAL   SOLD  THERE
HOPE   TWOS  SATED
```

39

```
RAPT   CASAS  SLED
OLIO   ALAMO  TERI
AGER   MARIN  RAIN
MAINSPRING    EPEE
SENATE   ESSAY
   DARES   TIMETO
MAJOR  DAMES   AIL
OPUS   CIGAR  CREE
REM   OUTER  LASSO
ESPRIT   SCRAM
  SALSA   IMPOSE
ALEC   BANKVAULTS
SOAK   ARULE  SLAT
ANTE   CODER  EIRE
PEST   KNEES  SEER
```

40

```
BALL   MALT  DARNS
ELEE   ODIE  ETONS
LONGGREEN    FEUER
TEASET    STALAG
   NAN   STASHED
GIBBERED   STERNO
AMUST  PAREE   IDO
MANA   MARIA  ODIN
IRK   ROLES  BREVE
NEEDED   DECLARES
STRIPER    SRA
  HARMON   ESTATE
ABIDE  SAFETYPIN
SALES  IHOP   REND
PALMS  NAGS   ODES
```

41

```
GIMME   ATTS    CAR
ASIAN   GRAPH   REO
SMARTCOOKIE    ARA
    TIL   TERR   CID
AFRICAN    REMAKES
BIO    ERAS   SIDE
ALLS   EDEN  TERRA
BELL   TIMED  AJAR
ATTIC  RIGA   LAND
   OMAN   SERF   CEO
TAPERED    BRINKER
ADD    OARS    ONA
MAE   BREADWINNER
ENS    STAVE  ACORN
ROK    OMEN   LYRES
```

42

```
ALEC   PAGE  RECAP
NOVA   ALES  OPERA
EMIT   SINS  SADAT
WALNUTGROVE    ABE
  ATONE    ITOR
PAMPER    HITACHI
ADA   SABLE  ASHEN
PUPS   LEARS  TENT
ALLES  ADDER   SIE
STEELER    RITTER
  SPAS   MAGNA
ELY   SPRUCEGOOSE
SARAH  ALMA   IBID
AMUSE  TEEN   SOME
UPPER  ASST   MEIN
```

43

```
DOSE   GARP  SIPES
IDOL   AREA  TRADE
NORA   DONT  ASPIN
GRAYPANTHER    END
    NAB    SAMPRAS
LONESOME   PART
APE   SUEDE  NOISE
SIMI   TOWER  AGES
HEELS  WIRES   EAT
   ALTO  NOCTURNE
TENSION    EIN
ELL  CHESHIRECAT
SLINK  ELEV   ALVA
LEONE  DORE   SEEN
ASNER  YEAR   YORK
```

44

```
SPED    SHAH   ALTO
CAPES  TOGA   BIAS
ATOLL  REAR   EZRA
DIXIECARTER    TOG
SOY    ELI  EMIRATE
   PINS    STAY
GOBI   FEN   ZILCH
ADEN   FRISK  SOAR
REACT   FAR   ERRS
  AURA    FROM
BARRELS  ANA   ADO
LIT   KATEJACKSON
ASHY   SAVE  HEIRS
SLUE   KIEV  OLDIE
TERN   ANNO   PEST
```

45

```
P I M A   M O S T   D E B T S
I R I S   E T T A   A L L I E
T A C K L E B O X   I L O N A
T E A S E T   A E O L I C
      A M O   S T I C K B Y
H A R S H E N S   T E E P E E
U S U R Y   S I L O S   A W L
B I N S   H E R O S   U R A L
E D T   S A T E S   E N T R E
R E H E E L   D E P L O Y E D
T S E T S E S   S A L
  S H A R I F   C A S H E S
I S H A M   K I C K S T A R T
C R O N E   H A V E   A R I A
H O W E S   S T I R   Y A N G
```

46

```
R A J A H   S C R A P   M A S
F L A M E   A L A N A   E L K
D A R Y L D R A G O N   R B I
      P R I M   C A V E D
S A L L I E S   C H A R G E S
T E E I N G   B O O K E R
O R A N G   W O R S E   I C H
R I F E   M I X E S   A F R O
Y E P   F I N E D   H I F I S
  H O A R D S   N U D I S T
I R O N I E S   L A M E N T S
S H E E R   A I D A
L O N   W O L F M A N J A C K
I D I   A R S O N   L O T T O
P A X   Y O U R S   Y E A R S
```

47

```
M A Y O   B R A E   S T O P
A R E A   F L O W N   L A D E
L O A F A R O U N D   I R O N
E M S   R O T E   O S C A R S
S A T U R N   S P R E E
      P A T H   A S T O U N D
W I S P Y   A C R E   F R A U
I D L E   B R A I D   L A I D
G E A R   R O B S   G I L L S
S A T C H E L   H A L F
      R E A D S   T E E N S Y
A M O U N T   H U L A   A N I
N A B S   H E E L A N D T O E
T R O T   E V A N S   E A R L
S E E S   R A R A   B L E D
```

48

```
P A R T S   S P I E L   R I P
O P E R A   C A R V E   A L I
T O B A C C O R O A D   I L L
      P R E T E N D   A L I A
A Y E   E L I   E R R A N T
L A R D   E A S T   A R T I E
P L I E R S   C A P R I
S U N S E T B O U L E V A R D
      S N E E R   A R A B I A
T O T E D   D E F Y   L U L L
A V E R S E   L L B   T E E
M I N T   N O S E E U M
A N S   S T R E E T S C E N E
L E E   T R E A T   E X T O L
E S S   Y E L L S   D I A R Y
```

49

```
L A D D   R A P S   W I C K S
A S I A   E D I E   I S L E T
M E N S   P O E M   G R A D E
B A T H T U B R I N G   S G T
      E R L E   E L O P E S
S A B R E S   A F R E S H
I W O   N E E D E D   L A B S
S E W E D   T O T   M O N E Y
I D L E   P A R A D E   D A N
  I N S O L E   A D E S T E
M A N S E S   E M I T
A L G   C H A R M S C H O O L
V A P O R   L U C E   A L M A
E M I L E   A B E L   N E A P
N O N E T   S E E S   E O N S
```

50

```
S A S S   C R U D E   S W A B
T A T E   H O S E S   H I R E
O R A L   E V E N T   E M I T
W O R L D S E R I E S   B A H
E N T E R S   M E T A L
      R E M I T   M O D E S T
M I S S   A R I D   R A D I O
A S U   A N I M A T E   O F T
P I P E R   S I T E   A N T E
S T E R O L   D E L O N
      R E M A N   E L I S H A
N A B   A M E R I C A S C U P
O B O E   E V I T A   E A R S
N E W T   N E R O S   E L L E
O L L A   T R E N T   D A Y S
```

51

```
B E A M   M A T S   P O S T S
A G R A   A M A T   O U T R E
R A I N   G A L L   S T A I N
I N D I A N S C O U T   G A T
      A V A S   P A M E L A
B A S S E T   F R O L I C
A S I   R E E L I N   T O I L
N I X E S   T I C   C E A S E
E A S T   S T E E L E   C E N
  H O L I E R   A L T H E A
A T O N A L   I D E A
T O O   C O W B O Y B O O T S
E N T R E   H A N D   I H O P
S T E E R   A R I A   S I N O
T O R T S   T R A Y   M O S T
```

52

```
H E L M   W A R E S   S P C A
O P I E   A B I D E   T O O L
B I A S   L U C I E   E N D S
C R O W D T H E P L A T E
      Z O O S   E L I S
B E L O W   A T H O S
A L A I   V I S I O N   P O I
C I R C L E T H E W A G O N S
H A D   E N T E R S   E L L E
B A T O N   A N E Y E
T H U S   N U D E
B I R T H D A Y P A R T Y
P O N D   M A L L E   A W A Y
I N G E   O R I O N   L I L I
E D E N   S T A N D   S T E P
```

53

```
A L M S   O V E R T   A B E L
T E E S   P A L E R   M O R T
B A S E B A L L D I A M O N D
E N S   A Q U A   F L A K E S
S T E   R U E   B L A N C
T O D A T E   G O E S   L O P
      P E S T E R S   A U R A
M I S E R   E T E   E L B O W
R O A D   O X I D A N T
S U M   P S A T   P L E N T Y
  S P A H N   E P I   U R E
R E P A C K   E L A N   M U S
H E A R T O F D A R K N E S S
E R D E   S L A T E   A R T E
A Y E S   H A M E L   B O Y D
```

54

```
A G R A   S H A D   R E B E L
H U E R   C A R E   I N U R E
A R E A   A L A S   A L L A N
B U F F A L O B I L L   L S D
      A L P S   I T C H E S
B A T T L E   S O N O R A
O U I   A L L E G E   E L B E
L E G G Y   A I R   R E S I N
O L E O   D I N E R O   E L I
  R E T I R E   O B E Y E D
D A W S O N   I M I N
R E O   W O L F M A N J A C K
A R O S E   A L A I   O T O E
F I D E L   S I G N   Y A L E
T E S T S   E P E E   S N A P
```

55

```
P A C T S   L I S P   D I P S
A F L A T   O T T O   A R L O
P L A C E   W A R M   B E A U
  P I N K E L E P H A N T S
T A T T O O   A S A   I T E
O U R   S P O O K   V I C E S
S R A S   E E K   B O G
H I P P O C R A T I C O A T H
  I N K   P A L   T R I M
C R A T E   B I B L E   M N O
H E S   A L L   E X E R T S
A W H A L E O F A T A L E
N A C L   G O O N   C I S C O
C R A M   A D I N   T A T E R
E D N A   L Y E S   A S S E S
```

56

```
L E N T     O H O H   A M P S
O L I O   B R U T E   B E A T
B U Z Z A L D R I N   E Z I O
A D E   L I S T O N   E Z R A
R E R O O T   S E P T A
      P U Z Z L E R S   N I B
H O P I   E E E   T H I N E
A P I N   D E A L T   A N D A
S I Z E R   V I I   R E O S
P E Z   E M B E Z Z L E
  A P P A L   Z A M B I A
P A P A   L A C T I C   R N S
E L I S   O Z Z I E S M I T H
A G E S   N E A P S   M A R E
S A S E   E R R S   E N O S
```